CINCINNATI
Chefs Cook Book

by William B. Struss

19 classic meals from the areas finest restaurants

Cover design by Rod Bussler

Special thanks to Russ McMinn, Nancy Kidd and Jane Harwood

ISBN: 0-935201-72-6

Now you can enjoy Cincinnati's best restaurants' cuisine in the comfort of your own home.

This is a cookbook for those who like to eat out but would love to take the great recipes they've experienced home with them. Whether you're a novice or accomplished chef, you'll enjoy creating a complete meal covering soups through desserts outlined in the pages of this cookbook that feature some of the finest restaurants in Cincinnati.

Open the book and discover recipes to tantalize the palate from establishments such as the China Gourmet, Lenhardt's, Pigall's French Restaurant, La Normandie, Delmonicoe's and more! With this wide selection, you'll be able to please all types of tastes and will have a collection of recipes you'll use over and over.

CONTENTS

Brandywine Inn

Dinner for Four

Coquilles St. Jacques à la Bruxellois

Soupe au Fromage

Sorbet aux Poires

Medaillon de Veau au Poireaux

Tarte aux Pommes Narmande

Wine:

with the scallops - Pouilly Fuisse - Louis Jadot
with the veal - Chablis - Henri Laroche

George Bernas, Chef

Brandywine Inn

The Brandywine Inn, in the village of Monroe, situated between West Chester and Middletown, is located in one of the area's oldest buildings. Initially constructed in 1850 as a hotel and tavern, this building served as the halfway point for stagecoach travel between Cincinnati and Dayton. When stagecoach travel was at its peak, many a weary traveler found rest in the Old Hotel, as it was then known. Refreshments were available in the hotel's tavern, the Red Onion. Its location on the Cincinnati Dayton Road helped to make the Old Hotel a social gathering point on weekends. Business flourished until the railroads were built and became the common mode of travel between Cincinnati and Dayton. Over the years the Old Hotel changed ownership many times. Eventually the guest rooms were converted to apartments while the tavern gave way to a small shop.

The Brandywine Inn began as an idea shared by George and Doris Bernas and their friend, Steve Morgan. Their goal was to create a haven for people who, like themselves, enjoyed fine dining in the European tradition in which dining constituted the event of the evening. The renovation of the building and the construction of the Brandywine Inn was largely accomplished by hand labor of the Bernases, Steve Morgan and a few friends.

The highly polished tables were handmade by owner George Bernas and are enhanced by comfortable Windsor chairs. The Brandywine Inn serves five-course prix fixe meals that are elegant and absolutely flawless in execution. Everything from the bread to the sorbet is made from scratch. The set menu changes every weekend; you can get on the mailing list that announces what will be offered for six weeks in a row.

"A recipe," says Bernas, "is like a computer. A bunch of tiny basic things but when you put them together, they're complex."

The Brandywine Inn is half way between Cincinnati and Dayton, one mile off the interstate. Take I-75 to the Monroe exit #29 and turn West onto Ohio Route 63. Proceed one mile to the first traffic light and turn left onto Main Street. Then just three blocks and turn left into the Brandywine Inn's parking lot. It is definitely worth the trip!

204 South Main Street
Monroe
(513) 539-8911 or (513) 793-4509

Coquilles St. Jacques à la Bruxellois

1 pound sea scallops
1 cup onion, finely chopped
4 fresh tomatoes, peeled, seeded
* and chopped*
3 tablespoons olive oil
1 cup grated Gruyere cheese

3 tablespoons butter
2 cloves garlic, finely
* chopped*
1/4 cup heavy cream
1 teaspoon thyme
1/4 cup flour

1. Clean sea scallops under cold running water and drain. In a 4 quart sauce pan add sea scallops and water to cover, bring just to boil and drain. Reserve the liquid.
2. In a 6 quart sauce pan, add oil and saute onion and garlic until soft. Add flour and cook 3 minutes, then add tomatoes, thyme and cook for 5 minutes. Add 1 cup reserved scallop liquid and heavy cream, simmer 10-15 minutes or until thick.
3. To serve place scallops in individual ramekins. Spoon stuffing over scallops, then top with grated cheese and sprinkle with melted butter. Bake at 350 degrees for 15 to 20 minutes until hot.

Soupe au Fromage
(A Hearty Cheese Soup)

1 pound potatoes, peeled
* and diced*
2 tablespoons butter
6 tablespoons cream
1/2 pound Swiss cheese, grated

6-1/2 cups water
1-1/2 teaspoons salt
1 pound onions
pepper to taste

1. Cut onions into large dice, then sweat onions in butter until soft. Add water, salt and potatoes, bring to boil and cook until potatoes are soft. Add cream, Swiss cheese and pepper to taste.

Sorbet aux Poires

1 pound fresh pears, cored
  and chopped
juice of one lemon

2 cups sugar
4 oz. egg whites

1. In a 6 quart sauce pan, put pears, sugar, lemon juice and water to cover. Bring to boil then simmer until pears are tender. Puree in blender and place in ice cream maker, until firm.
2. Beat egg whites until firm peaks, fold into the pears. Freeze overnight.

Medaillon de Veau au Poireaux

8 veal tenderloin steaks
1/2 cup bacon, chopped
1/2 cup butter
1/2 cup veal stock
salt and pepper

6 leeks, white and light green
  parts only
1/4 cup flour
1/4 cup sour cream

1. Cut or chop bacon, and render gently over heat. Take bacon out of pan, add butter and leeks. Gently cook the leeks until tender. To the leeks add flour, cook 5 minutes. Add veal stock and sour cream. Salt and pepper to taste. Add back the bacon and cook 10 minutes.
2. Heat 2 tablespoons butter in frying pan until it sizzles. Lightly salt and pepper the veal steaks and cook over low heat until golden brown.
3. To serve, top veal steaks with leek sauce and sprinkle with chopped parsley.

Vegetables: Buttered green beans and julienne of carrots.

Tarte aux Pommes Normande
(Sweet Tart Pastry)

1-1/4 cups unbleached flour
1 egg yolk
1/2 teaspoon salt

3 oz. butter
1/4 cup ground almonds
2 tablespoons cold water

1. Mix together flour, almonds, salt and sugar in mixing bowl. Add chilled butter, cut into small chunks and, with the tips of the fingers, quickly mix butter into dough until it forms large crumbs. Add egg yolk, then ice water, one tablespoon at a time, until the dough just holds together.

2. Turn out onto a lightly floured surface. Take an egg-sized portion of dough and push it across the surface with the heel of the hand. Repeat with the remainder of the dough and gather into a flattened ball. Cover and refrigerate 15 minutes. (Can be refrigerated 3 days or frozen.)

3. Roll out dough and line a 10 inch tart pan with removable bottom.

Filling

3 oz. butter, softened
1 egg plus 1 yolk
2/3 cup (100 g) blanched
*   almonds, ground*
3 or 4 Red or Gólden
*   Delicious apples*

1/2 cup sugar
1 tablespoon apple brandy or
*   orange liqueur*
2 tablespoons flour

1. Cream the butter, gradually add the sugar and beat until light. Beat in the eggs, liqueur, almonds and flour in order.

2. Meanwhile, blind bake the tart shell in a 350 degree oven (line with paper, fill with dried beans, and bake 10 minutes; remove beans and bake 5 minutes longer.)

3. Spread the almond filling into the cooled tart shell. Peel, core and halve the apples. Slice very thin. Flatten slice halves slightly and arrange on almond cream. Bake at 400 degrees for 15 minutes, then at 350 degrees another 20 minutes. Spread top with strained apricot jam.

Celestial Restaurant

Dinner for Four

Pate De Campagne

Creme D'Amande

Salade De Poreaux Vinaigrette

Loup de Mer Grillee Mousseline De Bearnaise

Cassatta A Ma Facon

Wine:

Edna Valley Chardonnay, 1985

Celestial Restaurant

The Celestial Restaurant occupies the spot once known for the Mt. Adams Incline and the Highland House, a famous restaurant, concert hall, and beer garden. Patrons enjoying the carved wood and exquisite details of its warm Hunt Club atmosphere are treated to an unprecedented view of downtown Cincinnati, the Ohio River with its newly developed riverfront, and the rolling hills of Kentucky. Under the leadership of Manager Robert Thorne and Chef de Cuisine Georges Pulver, the French and Continental cuisine combine with impeccable service to provide a world class dining experience.

1071 Celestial Street
(513) 721-5088

Pate De Campagne
(Country Pate)

1 pound pork shoulder	*1 pound pork liver*
1 pound ham (to add red	*1 pound pork fat or lard*
color to meat	*2 onions*
1 teaspoon fresh thyme	*1 bay leaf*
leaves	*1 clove garlic*
6 branches parsley	*1 tablespoon flour*
2 eggs	*salt and pepper to taste*

1. Grind all meat together with the onion, parsley, thyme, bay leaves and garlic. Add salt and pepper to taste. Add flour and eggs and mix everything together with your hands.
2. Line the bottom and sides of a 9 x 5 loaf pan with the slices of lard. Pack the meat mixture in the mold and cover with thin slices of lard. Bake in a bain-Marie at 325 degrees for one hour, 45 minutes. Remove from oven and pour hot liquid gelatin over the plate.
3. Chill overnight. Unmold onto cutting board. Slice loaf 1/2 inch thick. Trim any lard residue from outside edges and quarter slices. Serve with melba toast and cornichons.

Hot Liquid Gelatin

1 cup chicken stock	*2 teaspoons plain gelatin*

1. Sprinkle gelatin over cold chicken stock. Heat over low heat, stirring constantly until gelatin is completely dissolved.

Note: Extra servings keep well if wrapped tightly and refrigerated. Cutting the recipe in half or thirds would impair the quality of the dish.

Creme D'Amande
(Creme of Almond Soup)

6 cups chicken stock
1 cup half and half
4 egg yolks
chopped parsley
1-1/2 oz. Amaretto liqueur

1/2 pound ground, toasted
  almonds (can be finely
  ground in food processor)
salt and pepper to taste
sliced almonds for garnish

1. Bring stock to a boil and add almonds. Simmer 15 minutes. Beat together half and half with egg yolks. Whip this mixture into the stock and remove from heat.
2. Season to taste with salt and pepper. Add Amaretto, mixing well. Garnish with chopped parsley and sliced toasted almonds.
   Note: This soup is best when served immediately. However, it can be made ahead and reheated gently in double-boiler.

Salade De Poreaux Vinaigrette
(Leek Salad with Vinaigrette Dressing)

4 leeks (white part only)
4 teaspoons chopped onions
8 cherry tomatoes

8 oz. Vinaigrette dressing
  (your favorite)
16 branches parsley, chopped

1. Wash leeks thoroughly in cold water and cook in lightly salted water until crisp-tender. Drain and chill leeks. Place on cold salad plates and garnish with chopped parsley, onion and cherry tomatoes. Pass vinaigrette dressing on the side.

Loup De Mer Grillee Mousseline De Bearnaise

2 pounds sea bass filets
juice of 2 lemons

2 oz. melted sweet butter
salt and pepper to taste

1. Put melted butter in a baking pan just large enough to accommodate fish in one layer. Place fish in pan and turn to coat with butter. Pour lemon juice over fish; sprinkle with salt and pepper. Bake in preheated 350 degree oven for 5 - 6 minutes. Set fish aside and keep warm while preparing sauce.
2. Spread Mousseline sauce over the fish and place in broiler about 4 inches from heat until golden (probably less than 10 seconds).

Sauce Mousseline De Bearnaise
(Hollandaise Sauce)

4 egg yolks
1/2 oz. white wine
salt and pepper to taste

juice of one-half lemon
6 oz. melted sweet butter
tabasco sauce to taste (1-3 drops)

1. In a stainless steel bowl, mix egg yolks and white wine. Continue whisking over simmering water until mixture is thick and lemon colored. Add melted butter drop by drop, whisking constantly. When butter is thoroughly incorporated, stir in lemon juice, Tabasco, salt and pepper.

1 tablespoon dried tarragon leaves
1/2 cup red wine vinegar

1 oz. sweet butter
1/2 teaspoon chopped, dry shallots

1. Saute shallots in sweet butter until golden. Add tarragon leaves and wine vinegar. Simmer until vinegar has evaporated. Mix into Hollandaise sauce along with 2/3 cup whipped heavy cream.

Cassatta A Ma Facon
(Cake My Way)

2 cups heavy cream
1 16 oz. pound cake
1/2 cup strawberries
1/2 cup peaches
10 oz. Cointreau
generous, 1/2 cup toasted
*   slivered almonds*

1 cup sugar
1/2 cup bing cherries
1/2 cup raspberries
1/2 cup kiwi fruit
2 cups raspberry sherbet,
*   softened*
candied violets

1. Coarsely chop all the fruit and place in stainless steel bowl. Add Contreau and soak for 2 to 3 hours. Whip the cream with sugar until stiff. Place in refrigerator to keep chilled. Slice the pound cake horizontally into 4 thin layers. Drain chopped fruit, reserving the Contreau.

2. Place one layer of cake on a silver platter or serving plate. Cover with half the drained, chopped fruit. Add another layer of pound cake, cover with the remaining fruit. Add a third layer of pound cake and cover with the softened sherbet.

3. With the handle of a wooden spoon make 4 holes in the sherbet. Pour 1 tablespoon of the reserved Cointreau in each hole. Place fourth layer of pound cake on top of cake, extending ends to a point, forming a sort of boat shape. Cover top of cake with whipped cream. Sprinkle sides of cake with toasted almonds. Garnish with candied violets.

Champs

Dinner for Two

*Chilled Smoked Tenderloin with
Pommery Mustard Sauce*

Centerfield Salad

Lemon Sorbet Mini-Cones

Cajun Style Shrimp with Black Bean Sauce and Fresh

Dill Fettuccine

Flourless Chocolate Cake

Wine:

*with Tenderloin and Salad -
Cakebread Sauvignon Blanc, 1986*

with Shrimp - Grgich Hills Chardonnay, 1986

*with Chocolate Cake and Kona Coffee - Essencia
Orange Muscat Sweet Dessert Wine, 1986*

Champs

Champs restaurant, located on the Hyatt Regency Cincinnati's lobby level, combines understated elegance of the hotel with a sports motif, creating a somewhat casual steak and seafood house. The restaurant's name was derived from Cincinnati's rich heritage as "The City of Champions". The preparation of house specialties becomes the backdrop to an enjoyable evening.

Beginning as a great steak house in the best midwestern tradition, Champs has evolved into a forum for the freshest seafood, including live Maine lobster and American regional features as well. Custom dry-aged beef cut to order, a secret steak seasoning, fresh Lake Superior Walleye Pike and sausages, smoked fish and fresh pastas made on the premises are all hallmarks of the restaurant. The service is distinctly American too - servers are friendly and relaxed, but attentive to every detail and very knowledgeable about food and wines they present. The culinary staff and service personnel meet daily to discuss food preparation and special cooking techniques to be featured in the "show kitchen" that day.

Champs restaurant is a "cut above" the great American steak house, located at 151 West Fifth Street, Cincinnati, Ohio at Hyatt-Saks Fifth Avenue Center.

151 West Fifth Street
(513) 579-1234

Chilled Smoked Tenderloin
(with Pommery Mustard Sauce)

8 oz. well trimmed beef tenderloin with burgundy wine to cover hickory wood chips and/or sawdust.

2 tablespoons pickling spices (juniper berries, cloves, bay leaf, allspice, black pepper)

1. Pour wine over tenderloin until completely covered, add pickling spices and refrigerate over night.
2. The smoking process can be accomplished in two ways, as a cold or hot smoke. Our chef prefers the cold smoking method of placing the raw, marinated beef on a rack in a vented enclosed cabinet. In the bottom of the metal cabinet a few charcoal briquettes are kindled and allowed to burn until glowing and covered with white ash. At this point the meat is placed inside and the coals covered with two handfuls of hickory chips that have been soaked in water overnight and then one handful of fine hickory sawdust. The meat is smoked this way for two to three hours renewing the chips and sawdust when the smoke lessens. The temperature inside never exceeds 120 degrees F and the tenderloin remains raw and therefore most receptive to the smokey flavor. The meat is then removed and roasted in a 450 degree oven to a medium rare internal temperature of 150 degrees F.

   The same effect can be achieved at home with most gas or charcoal grills. The tenderloin is marinated as before and placed in a closed grill where soaked hickory chips are spread over the briquettes so that the meat is smoked and cooked at the same time.
3. Chill the tenderloin completely, slice thin and serve with Pommery mustard sauce and any combination of the following chilled garnishes:
   - Spicy alfalfa sprouts
   - Cornichons (small marinated gherkins)
   - Sun-dried tomatoes
   - Oil cured olives
   - Julienned daikon (oriental radish)

Pommery Mustard Sauce

1/2 cup sour cream
1 teaspoon Dijon Mustard
1/2 teaspoon lemon juice

salt to taste
1-1/2 tablespoon Pommery mustard
pinch Cayenne pepper

Centerfield Salad

1/2 pound fresh spinach
1/2 cup shredded smoked
  mozzerella cheese

1/4 head napa (oriental
  cabbage)
2 heaping tablespoons pine
  nuts, toasted

1. Remove stems from spinach leaves, rinse and drain thoroughly. Chop or tear leaves into bite sized pieces.
2. Shred the napa finely and combine with spinach.
3. Toss the greens with the raspberry vinagrette just before service and garnish with the shredded cheese and pine nuts.

Raspberry-Mint Vinagrette

1/2 cup raspberry preserves
1/2 cup dry white wine
4 tablespoons white vinegar
1/4 cup (scant) olive oil

1/2 cup fresh spearmint
  leaves
1 teaspoon lime zest

1. Combine all ingredients except olive oil in a sauce pot. Bring to boil then simmer slowly for ten to fifteen minutes to extract the mint flavor.
2. Strain the mixture through cheese cloth and cool to room temperature.
3. Whisk in olive oil and add salt and pepper to taste.
   The Champs crew encourages guests to enjoy a palate cleanser between salad and entree. We present a miniature ice cream cone with a small scoop of lemon ice for this purpose. It is our answer to the French sorbet course.

Cajun Style Shrimp
(with black Bean Sauce)

14 pieces raw, headless U-15*
   shrimp (*Less than 15 per lb.)
1/2 cup dry white wine

2 tablespoons unsalted
   butter
1-2 teaspoons Cajun
   seasoning mixture

1. Peel and devein shrimp, if necessary, leaving tails on for appearance.
2. Saute shrimp in butter, adding cajun seasoning mixture to taste (we like it hot!) until nearly done. Add white wine to pan, cooking for an additional minute or so to allow the alcohol to evaporate. Be careful not to overcook the shrimp.
3. Remove shrimp from pan, arranging seven per entree on top of black bean sauce. Garnish with sour cream and fresh cilantro.

Cajun Seasoning Mixture

1 teaspoon Hungarian paprika
1/2 teaspoon granulated onion
1/2 teaspoon ground black
   pepper
1/2 teaspoon oregano leaves

1/3 teaspoon salt
1/2 teaspoon granulated
   garlic
1/2 teaspoon thyme leaves

Black Bean Sauce

1 cup dry black turtle beans
2-3 cups chicken broth
1 or 2 fresh jalepeno peppers,
  minced
1/3 cup diced crisp bacon, diced
prosciutto ham, or cooked
chorizo sausage (hot Spanish
  style sausage)

Water to cover
2/3 cup diced fresh tomato
1/3 cup spanish onion,
  minced
2 tablespoons fresh chopped
  cilantro leaves
Cajun Seasoning mix to taste

1. Pick through and rinse beans, cover with cold water and refrigerate overnight.
2. Combine 2 cups of beans (they expand with soaking) with chicken broth, tomato and jalepeno pepper, bring to a boil, then simmer gently for 1 to 1/2 hours.
3. While simmering, saute onions until soft, with bacon, ham or sausage and add to the above.
4. The sauce will be completed when the mixture is thick and beans are soft. At this time, season to taste with cajun spice mixture and fresh cilantro.

Fresh Dill Fettuccine

3/4 cup all purpose flour   1 egg
1/4 teaspoon salt   1/2 tablespoon olive oil
1/4 tablespoon luke warm water 1 tablespoon fresh dill weed

1. Place the flour in a bowl forming a well in the center. Break the egg into the well and add the other ingredients. With a wooden fork or whisk, beat the egg and incorporate flour into the wet ingredients from the inside out. If the dough seems sticky, add a little more flour. Form the dough into a ball and knead it for about five minutes. Rest, covered, for fifteen minutes.

2. Roll out pasta to approximately 1/8 inch thick, either by hand with a rolling pin or a pasta machine may be used. Cut fettuccine about 1/4 inch wide.

3. Cook pasta in lots of boiling salted water to the "al dente" stage - firm to the bite. Drain and combine in saute pan with the roasted red pepper cream sauce and perhaps, some chopped fresh scallion and ripe olives for garnish. Heat thoroughly and serve in heated side dish.

Roasted Red Pepper Cream Sauce

1 red bell pepper, medium
  sized
1/2 teaspoon coarsley ground
  black pepper
salt to taste

2 cups heavy cream
1 clove fresh garlic,
  minced finely
2 tablespoons freshly
  grated Parmesan cheese

1. Place the pepper under a broiler four to six inches from the heat source to blacken the skin. Turn the pepper so that the entire surface is charred. The same result may be achieved by holding the pepper over an open flame. Once roasted, plunge the pepper into ice water to loosen the skin. Peel the charred skin off and split the pepper in half. Now remove all seeds, membrane and the stem. Puree the remainder in a food processor until liquid.

2. Combine the pepper puree, cream, garlic and black pepper in a heavy sauce pan and bring to a boil. Simmer the mixture at medium heat, stirring often, until slightly thickened, or until it is reduced by one third. Stir in the grated Parmesan and check to see if salt or additonal black pepper is needed.

3. Combine fettuccine and vegetable garnishes and heat through.

   In addition to choosing baked potato, rice or fresh pasta, our guests are treated to two types of vegetables with their entree presentation. May we suggest ginger and honey glazed carrots and a sauteed medley of snow peas, yellow summer squash, tomato juliennes and fresh garlic?

Flourless Chocolate Cake

*1 pound semi-sweet dark
    chocolate
1/2 pound unsalted butter,
    softened*

*2 cups granulated sugar
1/2 cup brewed coffee
8 eggs, beaten
2 tablespoons Frangelica or
    liqueur of choice*

1. Melt chocolate, sugar and coffee in double boiler stirring occasionally. When completely melted, remove from heat and add butter, eggs and liquer. Mix until smooth and creamy.
2. Pour batter in a 10 inch cake pan lined with aluminum foil and greased. Bake in 350 degree oven for 1 hour to 1 hour and fifteen minutes. The cake will set but still be soft when done. (The toothpick test does no work on this cake).
3. Refrigerate the cake overnight or until completely cool. Turn cake out onto a plate, peel off aluminum foil and turn back over onto serving plate. Dust with powdered sugar or chocolate shavings and serve with whipped cream.

Yields ten to twelve serious chocolate servings!

Chester's Roadhouse

Dinner for Six

Wild Mushroom Torte

*Beef Consomme with Diced Vegetables
and Cheese Straw*

Salad with Italian Chicken Strips and Honey Sauce

Sauteed Scallops and Shrimp with Garlic Potatoes

Fresh Snow Peas Provencale

*Fresh Raspberry Crepe with Pastry Creme
and Chocolate Lace*

Menu prepared by Chef Alain Peyron

Chester's Roadhouse

This charming old farmhouse turned roadhouse turned greenhouse is a great place to dine in Cincinnati. The bar is special. Relax with a drink on the front porch. Make your own salad, and watch the chef prepare daily specials, prime rib, baby rack of lamb, steaks, lobster and an array of fresh fish and vegetables every day. After spending nine years, among many other accomplishments, as the sous chef at the Maisonette - The Comisar Family's flagship restaurant - Chef Alain Peyron is pleased to be lending his culinary expertise to the American cuisine at Chester's Roadhouse. Entertainment Sunday through Friday is subtle. Lunch weekdays; dinner, seven nights. Reservations.

9678 Montgomery Road, (513) 793-8700
Mark Rafferty, General Manager

Wild Mushroom Torte

Crepe:
1 cup flour
2-1/2 oz. butter

1-1/2 cups milk
3 eggs

1. Combine milk and egg and flour in mixing bowl. Brown butter on medium low heat and add to batter. Let batter rest for 1 hour. Makes 25-27 crepes. Cut crepes down to 4 inch diameter with cookie cutter.

Sauce:
3 shallots, diced
4 tomatoes, peeled, seeded, and diced

1 cup sherry
10 green peppercorns, crushed
2 cups heavy cream

1. Cook sherry, shallots, green peppers and cream. Reduce to thickness. Add tomatoes. Keep warm.

Filling:
1 pound 2 oz. shitake mushrooms, chopped
1 pound 8 oz. enoki mushrooms, chopped (6 oz. for garnish)
2 tablespoons tarragon
4 oz. butter

1 pound 2 oz. button mushrooms chopped
1 pound 2 oz. oyster mushrooms chopped
2 tablespoons chervil, chopped

1. Saute in butter all mushrooms (except 6 oz. of enoki for garnish), chervil and tarragon for 1 - 1-1/2 minutes. Salt and pepper to taste. Put 2 oz. of sauce on 6 inch plate. Place 1 crepe over sauce and continue to build torte; 1 oz. mushrooms, 1 crepe; 1 oz. mushrooms, 1 crepe; 1 oz. mushrooms, 1 crepe. Garnish with enoki mushrooms.

Cheese Straw

1 cup ground romano
1/2 oz. paprika

1 cup ground parmesan
3 sheets prepared puff pastry
(dough sheets 5" x 5")

1. Mix romano, parmesan and paprika. Cut puff 1" x 5" long. Dip puff in egg and roll in cheese mixture. Twist to form a spiral and bake at 375 degrees for 8 to 10 minutes. Keep warm.

Beef Consomme with Diced Vegetables

3 quarts water
2 carrots, diced
2 onions, diced
1 bay leaf
1 cup mushrooms, diced
1 oz. yellow squash, diced
1 oz. zucchini, diced
1 oz. yellow corn

4 pounds beef bones, washed
in cold water
2 stalk celery, diced
pinch of thyme
8 egg whites
1 oz. red pepper, diced
1 oz. asparagus, diced

1. Place beef, water, 1 carrot, 1 onion, 1 stalk celery, bay leaf, thyme, mushrooms and leek in stock pot. Bring to a slow simmer and continue to simmer for 4 hours uncovered. Strain beef stock and remove fat from the surface.
2. Place beef stock into stock pot and add 1 carrot, 1 onion, and 1 stalk celery (all finely chopped) and add beaten egg whites. Simmer slowly for 1-1/2 hours. Strain consomme through several thicknesses of cheesecloth or coffee filter. Keep warm.
3. Add asparagus, yellow squash, zucchini, red pepper, yellow corn, and salt and pepper to taste. Serve very hot in 5 oz. soup bowl with cheese straw on side.

Salad with Italian Chicken Strips and Honey Sauce

Honey Dressing:
3 tablespoons honey
2 tablespoons Dijon mustard
1/4 cup red wine vinegar

1-1/2 cups salad oil
4 tablespoons country Dijon
  mustard
salt and pepper to taste

1. Mix all ingredients and leave at room temperature.

Chicken Strips:
8 oz. bread crumbs
1 teaspoon basil
2 eggs, lightly beaten

3 6 oz. chicken breasts,
  skinned
1 teaspoon granulated garlic

1. Mix bread crumbs, basil, garlic and oregano. Cut chicken breasts 1/2 to 2" long. Dip in egg. Roll in seasoned bread crumbs. Deep fry at 350 degrees until golden brown.

Salad:
1 small head romaine lettuce,
  chopped in 1" pieces
1 bunch watercress, cleaned
12 cherry tomatoes

1 head iceburg lettuce,
  chopped in 1" pieces
1/2 head red cabbage,
  julienned

1. Mix all salad ingredients except tomatoes. Add dressing and mix. Divide on six salad plates. Top with chicken strips and garnish with cherry tomatoes.

Sauteed Scallops and Shrimp with Garlic Potatoes

Sauce:
3-1/2 cups mushrooms, julienned
   (shitake and oyster)
1 oz. butter

2 large leeks, julienned
   (white part only)
3-1/2 cups heavy cream

1. Saute leek and mushrooms in butter over medium heat for 2 minutes. Add cream and cook over low heat for 4 minutes or until cream has thickened. Set aside and keep warm.

Garlic Potatoes:
10 whole cloves garlic, peeled,
1/4 cup heavy cream
1 oz. salad oil

3 pounds baking potatoes
   peeled and diced
6 oz. butter

1. Saute garlic in oil until golden. Place garlic in blender until smooth. Cook potatoes in water until soft. Drain potatoes and hold in large bowl.
2. Warm cream and butter. Add cream, butter and garlic to potatoes and whip. Add salt and pepper to taste.

Scallops and Shrimp:
1 pound (36-40) shrimp,
   peeled and deveined

1 pound bay scallops
1 oz. salad oil

1. Saute scallops and shrimp in oil over high heat for 1 to 2 minutes. Add sauce and reduce for 30 seconds. Make a nest with garlic potatoes on six 8″ plates. Place scallops and shrimp inside nest of potatoes.

Snow Peas Provencale

1 pound snow peas, cleaned
1 oz. olive oil
1 teaspoon parsley, finely
  chopped

3 large tomatoes
2 cloves garlic, finely
  chopped
1 oz. onion, chopped

1. Scald tomatoes for 1 minute, then peel, seed and finely chop. On medium heat, saute onion, 1/2 of the garlic and 1/2 of the olive oil for 1 minute. Add tomato and parsley. Cook for 2 minutes. Set aside and keep warm.
2. On medium heat saute snow peas in remaining olive oil and garlic for 30-60 seconds. Divide tomato mixture on six 4″ plates and top with snow peas.

Fresh Raspberry Crepe
with Pastry Creme and Chocolate Lace

Crepe Batter:
1/3 cup flour
2 tablespoons butter
8" skillet or crepe pan

1/2 cup milk
1 egg
1 teaspoon sugar

1. Combine milk, egg, flour and sugar in mixing bowl. Brown butter on medium low heat and add to batter. Let batter rest one hour. Make six thin crepes.

Chocolate Sauce:
1-1/2 cups milk
1/4 cup sugar

10 oz. semi sweet chocolate
chopped fine

1. Over medium heat in double boiler mix chocolate, milk and sugar. Stir until chocolate is melted. Keep at room temperature.

Pastry Creme:
1/2 teaspoon vanilla
2/3 cup sugar

2 cups milk
6 eggs, lightly beaten
3 tablespoons cornstarch

1. Combine 1/2 cup milk and cornstarch; add eggs. Combine 1-1/2 cups milk, vanilla and sugar in saucepan and cook over medium heat. Bring to a boil while stirring frequently.
2. Add cornstarch mixture, stirring constantly, until boiling and remove from heat. Keep at room temperature.

Filling: *6 pints fresh red raspberries*

1. Lay out crepe and fill with 1/2 cup red raspberries. Roll up and place on 6" plate.
2. Top crepe with 2 oz. pastry creme.
3. Lace with chocolate sauce and garnish with fresh whipped cream and mint leaf.

China Gourmet

Dinner for Four

Hot and Sour Soup

Wonderful Taste Chicken

Steamed Prawns with Black Bean Sauce

Beverage:

Tsingtao Beer

China Gourmet

Bing Moy is the essence of China Gourmet. He is a relaxed and gracious host who knows how to prepare the most delicious and exquisite food, and that is really what is most important to him. He is very serious about good food, and it shows. The fabulous menu boasts dishes from Canton, Hunan and Szechwan, however, a majority of Bing's customers order directly from the kitchen.

China Gourmet is located in Hyde Park and has been voted "consistently best" by Cincinnati Magazine for the past twelve years. It is listed in the Mobil Travel Guide and is an award winning restaurant.

3340 Erie Avenue, (513) 871-6612

Hot and Sour Soup

1 quart good chicken broth
2 oz. bean curd, shredded
2 tablespoons bamboo shoots,
  shredded
2 tablespoons dry lily buds
1 teaspoon salt
1 teaspoon sugar
3 tablespoons white cider or
  rice wine vinegar
1 egg, beaten
few drops sesame oil

2 oz. raw pork tenderloin,
  shredded
2 tablespoons fungus,
  shredded
1 tablespoon fresh ground
  black pepper
1 tablespoon dark soy sauce
2-3 teaspoons cornstarch
  dissolved in 2 tablespoons
  water
2 tablespoons minced green
  onions or scallions

1. In a heavy kettle, bring the broth to a boil. Meanwhile soften the shredded fungus and dry lily buds in water to cover. Drain well. Add the pork, bean curd, bamboo shoots, fungus and lily buds to the boiling stock. Bring again to a boil and stir in the pepper, salt, sugar, soy sauce and vinegar.
2. Slowly stir in the dissolved cornstarch until desired thickness. Slowly pour the beaten egg into the soup, whisking constantly to form thin strands of egg. Remove from heat and add oil. Ladle into bowls and garnish with minced scallions.

Wonderful Taste Chicken

2 whole chicken breasts, boned
Steam chicken until tender.

Sauce

1 teaspoon fresh ground pepper
1 tablespoon green scallions,
finely chopped
shredded chili pepper to taste*
1 tablespoon sesame oil
1 tablespoon sugar

1 tablespoon fresh ginger
root, finely chopped
1 clove garlic, minced
1 tablespoon sesame paste
4 tablespoons soy sauce
1 tablespoon vinegar

1. In a mixing bowl, combine all sauce ingredients. Pour over steamed chicken. Serve with steamed rice.
   *Note: Bing Moy suggests 1 tablespoon shredded chili pepper.

Steamed Prawns with Black Bean Sauce

12-16 prawns (shrimp), clean,
peel, devein and butterfly
3 scallions, trimmed and
shredded

1 tablespoon black soy beans,
cleaned and mashed
4 teaspoons peanut oil
1 tablespoon (optional to
taste) red chili pepper,
chopped and shredded

1. Arrange the prawns in a dish and arrange the shredded scallions, a dab of the mashed black beans, and shredded chili pepper to taste on top of each butterflied shrimp. Set the dish on a rack in a steamer and steam over high heat for 5 minutes. Remove from the steamer.
2. Heat peanut oil in wok and heat until oil is smoking. Drizzle hot oil over steamed prawns and serve at once.

Delmonico's

Dinner for Four

Alaskan Salmon Hash with Cilantro Butter Sauce

Johann Strauss Salad

*Roasted Veal & Lobster with Red Pepper &
Watercress Sauces*

Cream Brellee

Delmonico's

Delmonico's, overlooking Cincinnati's historic Fountain square, is located in The Westin Hotel. The famed Tyler Davidson Fountain, exquisitely lit at night, offers a romantic setting for a fine dining experience. Delmonico's features American gourmet cuisine served in an elegant and relaxing atmosphere.

Delmonico's is patterned after the famous Delmonico's Restaurant of Philadelphia from the late 1800's, known for using the finest ingredients. Today, Delmonico's, in the Westin Hotel, practices the same philosophy by including the best and freshest ingredients in the preparation of every menu item. Like the grand dining rooms of yesteryear, Delmonico's continues the tradition of offering the finest of food in an elegant setting.

Delmonico's kitchen staff is directed by Chef Robert Sturm, a graduate of Le Varrenne Ecole de Cuisine in Paris. Before returning to his native town of Cincinnati, Chef Sturm perfected his culinary art while serving world-renowned restaurants as Maxim's in Paris. "We practice the Old World methods," says Chef Sturm. "Fresh is best, so we start with quality ingredients prepared daily for each evening's service."

Open for dinner every night of the week, Delmonico's is a world-class experience, from the fine food and service to a complimentary rose for every lady. Reservations are required during the holiday season when lunch is served in addition to dinner, and recommended the rest of the year.

Alaskan Salmon Hash with Cilantro Butter Sauce

8 oz. poached salmon, cold
3 tablespoons onion, finely
  chopped
1/2 teaspoon ground cumin
2 tablespoons bread crumbs

4 oz. hash brown potato, raw
1 tablespoon fresh cilantro,
  chopped
1 egg
salt and pepper to taste

1. Mix all ingredients together and form into eight patties. Dredge each patty in flour and brown in a saute pan. Keep warm.

Sauce Cilantro

1 tablespoon chopped shallots
2 tablespoons chopped cilantro
4 tablespoons whole butter, soft

1 teaspoon chopped garlic
2 cups whipping cream

1. Mix shallots, garlic, cilantro and cream together. Reduce by 1/2, slowly boiling cream. Whip in soft butter a little at a time. Keep warm until service.

Johann Strauss Salad

8 oz. spinach, fresh
1 cup croutons, herbal
2 oz. Pernod liquor

4 oz. bacon strips, diced
4 eggs, hard boiled, chopped
2 cups gourmet dressing

1. Saute bacon and flame with Pernod liquor, (highly flammable, be careful). Add to a bowl containing spinach and croutons. Toss together with dressing, and put on a plate. Top each with chopped egg.

Gourmet Dressing

1 cup olive oil
1 tablespoon black pepper, ground
1 tablespoon chopped chives
1/2 tablespoon Lea & Perrin Worcestershire sauce
1 egg

1/2 cup terragon vinegar
1/2 tablespoon salt
1 tablespoon Dijon mustard
2 tablespoons parsley, chopped
juice of 1 lemon
4 drops tabasco sauce

1. In a bowl, whip mustard, egg, lemon juice and salt together. Slowly pour in olive oil while whipping. Then add the vinegar. Add all other ingredients and chill.

Roasted Veal & Lobster
(with Red Pepper and Watercress Sauce)

1 veal loin, cut in half
across the width

2 8 oz. lobster tails,
shelled, raw

1. Poke a hole through the length of the veal loin and force raw lobster tail into hole so that it fills the center of the loin. Roast until 135 degrees F. Slice each roast in 6 slices.

Red Pepper Sauce

2 red bell peppers
2 cups cream

1 cup Chablis wine
salt and pepper

1. Seed peppers, and roast until skin blisters. Peel peppers and puree in food processor. Place pepper in saucepan with white wine, and reduce until slightly thick. Add cream and reduce again until thick - Keep warm. Season with salt and pepper.

Watercress Sauce

1 bunch watercress
2 cups cream

1 cup Chablis wine
salt and pepper

1. Puree watercress with wine. Put in saucepan and follow the same direction for red pepper sauce.
2. Serve veal and lobster slices with your favorite pasta and the two sauces.

Cream Brellee

12 egg yolks
1 oz. pure vanilla extract

1 cup sugar
1 quart cream

1. Mix yolks and sugar in a bowl. Heat cream and vanilla extract together but do not boil. Slowly pour hot cream into yolk while stirring. Pour custard into four 6 ounce custard cups. Bake in a water bath for 35-40 minutes at 350 degrees F., or until custard has set like jello. Let cool - serve chilled.

The Heritage Restaurant

Dinner for Four

Cajun Barbecued Shrimp

Toasted Goat Cheese with Salad

Chicken Breast with Tarragon Cream Sauce

Jerry Hart's Chocolate Truffles

Wine:

With the Shrimp - cold beer or a feisty Zinfandel
With the Goat Cheese - a fresh Chenin Blanc
With the Chicken - full-bodied Cabernet Sauvignon or
a buttery Chardonnay

The Heritage Restaurant

The Heritage Restaurant is located in a pleasant country setting a dozen miles east of Cincinnati. The building itself is a restored 1827 manor house, converted to a restaurant at the turn of the century. It has been our pleasure to operate The Heritage since 1959. Through careful restoration the original ambiance of the individual rooms has been maintained to create the warmth and elegance of a bygone era. The grounds include award-winning herb and flower gardens that contain culinary, fragrant, ornamental herbs and perennial flowers that are used to decorate the tables as well as add freshness to the recipes.

The Heritage has been noted for its innovative interpretation of dining trends to satisfy the more sophisticated and adventuresome palates of the dining public. Heritage guests have always looked forward to their favorite restaurant for something new, yet worthwhile, along with many of the old time favorites.

The breakthroughs have been numerous. The Heritage was first to introduce Cincinnatians to French Nouvelle Cuisine, which has since given way to new Regional America Cooking. Teamed up with local wildlife artist John Ruthven, we were first to offer free-range "Chickens from Scratch" to area diners. A full five years before the Cajun craze swept the nation, The Heritage brought blackened redfish to the midwest. We have featured two popular festivals which create interest during the year - the Wild Game Festival, with such appetizers as safari samplers, and the Sophisticated Southwestern Festival, which is a continuing adventure into regional America specialties.

7664 Wooster Pike, (513) 561-9300
Janet and Howard Melvin

Cajun Barbecued Shrimp

1 cup vegetable oil
1 cup butter
1-1/2 tablespoons freshly ground
  black pepper
2 teaspoons dried rosemary,
  crushed
3 bay leaves, crushed
1 teaspoon Heritage Cajun
  Seafood Seasoning
1/2 teaspoon cayenne pepper
1/2 teaspoon dried oregano

1/2 teaspoon dried basil
1 tablespoon hot Hungarian
  paprika*
1/2 teaspoon salt
2 garlic cloves, finely minced
2 tablespoons catsup
1 tablespoon Worcestershire
  sauce
3 pounds raw shrimp-in-the-
  shell, peeled, leaving tail on
  (large: 18-20 count)
2 long loaves of French bread

1. Melt butter in a cast iron or heavy, oven proof skillet. Add the oil. Add the herbs and spices. Simmer over low heat for 10 minutes, stirring occasionally.
2. Add shrimp; cook for 2 minutes. Bake in a 425 degree oven 10-12 minutes, turning the shrimp once. Be careful not to overcook.
3. Serve with French bread.

   *Note: Hot Hungarian paprika is available at food specialty shops. Regular Hungarian paprika may be substituted if the hot is not available.

   The secret's out! After numerous trips to New Orleans in the name of research and many parties after Bengal games, we perfected our Cajun Barbecued Shrimp. We never had a problem with the attendance at the shrimp-tasting events. The shrimp are very spicy and wonderful. We have been told by some friends and customers that the bread dipped in sauce is almost better than the shrimp. Until this time, this recipe has been top secret. Enjoy!

Toasted Goat Cheese with Salad

8-10 ounces goat cheese
(Montrachet - log shaped) cut
into 16 slices, about 1/2" thick
1 egg
1 tablespoon water
1 teaspoon fresh thyme, finely
chopped (or 1 teaspoon dried)
1 teaspoon fresh oregano finely
chopped (or 1/3 teaspoon dried)
1/4 teaspoon salt

1 cup olive oil
1 tablespoon fresh thyme
leaves, chopped (or 1
teaspoon dried)
1 cup fresh bread crumbs
(dried may be substituted)
1 teaspoon fresh tarragon
finely chopped (or 1/3
teaspoon dried)
1/8 teaspoon freshly ground
pepper

1. Combine olive oil and thyme leaves. Coat goat cheese slices with oil mixture. Marinate 8 hours.
2. Combine egg and water in bowl. Beat slightly until combined. Mix bread crumbs and herbs, salt and pepper. Remove cheese from oil mixture. Dip cheese slices into the egg mixture and then into the bread crumbs. Place on an oiled or nonstick baking sheet and refrigerate.
3. Combine vinaigrette ingredients in bowl; whisk until blended. Prepare salad greens. Preheat oven to 400 degrees. Bake goat cheese rounds 6-10 minutes until golden. Toss greens with vinaigrette. Place on salad plates. Top each serving with two rounds of goat cheese.

Variations: Add chopped dried tomatoes, Greek olives, or sliced hearts of palm. The toasted goat cheese rounds may be served as an hors d'oeuvre with melba toast. Serve the rounds as an accompaniment to roasted or grilled meats. Domestic goat cheese is now available from Kentucky, Vermont and West Virginia.

Vinaigrette

oil from the cheese marinade
3 tablespoons Balsamic vinegar
salt and pepper to taste

selection of salad greens:
bibb, watercress, red leaf lettuce,
Belgian endive, or your choice

An exciting addition to salads or a great hors d'oeuvre. Montrachet goat cheese (log shaped) works the best, although different shapes of cheese can be used. In the summer, thyme blossoms can be used as a garnish.

Chicken Breast with Tarragon Cream Sauce

2 large chicken breasts, boned and halved
2 tablespoons green onions, finely chopped
2 tablespoons chives, finely chopped
1 cup Tarragon Cream Sauce (recipe follows)

1/4 cup butter (divided)
1/4 cup finely chopped shallots
2 tablespoons fresh parsley, finely chopped
salt and pepper to taste
2 teaspoons fresh tarragon, for garnish

1. Combine 2 tablespoons of the butter with the shallots, parsley, green onions and chives in a small bowl. Blend well and stuff 1/4 of the mixture underneath the skin of each chicken breast. Sprinkle the chicken breasts with salt and pepper to taste.
2. Heat remaining butter in a large skillet. Add the chicken breasts, skin-side down. Saute for 1 minute. Place breasts, skin-side up, in an ovenproof casserole along with the drippings from the skillet.
3. Bake in a 400 degree oven, 8-10 minutes. Serve with Tarragon Cream Sauce (recipe follows) and garnish with chopped tarragon.

Tarragon Cream Sauce

1 tablespoon butter
1/2 cup dry white wine
1 bay leaf
1 tablespoon fresh tarragon
salt to taste
pinch of freshly ground pepper
1 cup whipping cream

1/2 cup finely chopped
  shallots
1/2 teaspoon fresh thyme,
  chopped (or 1/8 teaspoon
  dried)
1/2 cup chicken stock,
  preferably homemade

1. Melt butter in a saucepan. When the butter is hot, add shallots. Cook, stirring, until the shallots are tender but not browned.
2. Add the wine, bay leaf, thyme, tarragon, salt and pepper. Cook until the wine is almost evaporated. Add the chicken broth and cook until the liquid is syrupy. Add the cream and cook over medium high heat, stirring, for 5 minutes until it has reduced to about 1 cup. Be careful not to let the cream boil over. Strain the sauce.

Yield: 1 cup

Note: Fresh herbs do make the difference. But in this case, if you can't find the fresh herbs, you can use dried herbs and produce a meal that is a very close second.

Jerry Hart's Chocolate Truffles
(Death by Chocolate)

*1 pound good quality semi-
sweet chocolate, chopped into
1/2 inch pieces*

1 cup whipping cream

1. Put chopped chocolate into a food processor. Bring whipping cream to a boil in a saucepan. Add hot cream to the chocolate.
2. Process until chocolate and cream mixture is smooth. Flavor with desired liqueur.
3. Cool and form into one inch balls.

Variations

Flavor with:
- One ounce Amaretto and roll in chopped, toasted almonds.
- One ounce Grand Marnier and one teaspoon grated orange rind, roll in cocoa powder.
- One ounce Kahlua and roll in a mixture of cocoa powder and a small amount of instant coffee.
- One ounce Frangelico and rolled in chopped, toasted hazelnuts.

Chef Hart is a chocoholic by his own admission. These truffles are heavenly and so simple to make and they can be made in so many flavors. Truffles make a terrific gift.

Iron Horse Inn

Dinner for Four

Iron Horse Inn Lobster Bisque

Iron Horse Inn Smoked Salmon Fettuccine

Iron Horse Inn

On Glendale's Village Square sits quaint little shops and an historical depot. The center of attraction is the old Brocker mansion, which is now the Iron Horse Inn. The Inn sits along the railroad tracks which were once a cattle run (as early as 1839, but certainly before 1856) from Hamilton, Ohio to the downtown Cincinnati stock yards.

A handsome, square, two story brick building, altered over the years, it has retained its bracketed gable roof and all of its original design. As the Iron Horse Inn, it continues a long tradition of serving the finest of food and drink to its patrons.

There is a comfortable "Mother Hubbard" atmosphere at the Iron Horse which takes its logo from the 1956 steam engine. Photographs, rich oil paintings and artifacts from Glendale's past carry out a subdued railroad motif, complimenting the brown, black and butterscotch decor in the two downstairs dining rooms.

Owners Dewey and Betty Huff have brought it to new culinary heights, earning three stars from the Mobil people in less than three years.

Everything is made from scratch, stocks are simmered for eighteen hours. Our beef items (steaks, etc.), are cut daily. Other specialties are roast duckling with orange sauce, chicken breast with chicken mousse and julienne vegetables and veal medallions with Chanterelle mushrooms and artichoke bottoms. All desserts are home baked along with our luncheon and dinner rolls.

Our menu maintains its rating as the finest in Cincinnati.

40 Village Square, Glendale, (513) 771-2050

Iron Horse Inn Lobster Bisque

4 medium lobster bodies	1 yellow onion, quartered
1 bunch celery, tops and leaves	1 teaspoon rosemary
1 teaspoon thyme	1-1/2 gallons spring water
1 cup tomato puree	2 cups heavy cream
1/2 cup clarified butter	1-1/2 cups flour
1/2 cup dry sherry wine	
(use the best)	

1. In a large oven proof pot, roast lobster bodies at 375 degrees for 30 minutes. Remove from oven and place over burner. Add onion, celery, bay leaves, herbs and water. Bring to a boil, reduce heat and simmer 45 minutes.
2. Lift out lobster bodies and discard. Whisk in tomato puree and cream. Blend clarified butter and flour to a paste; pinch bits of this off and whisk into soup to thicken to the consistency of creamy salad dressing. Add sherry just before serving. Strain through fine cheese cloth.

Iron Horse Inn Smoked Salmon Fettucine
(for Four)

1/2 cup white wine	4 cups pre-cooked fettucine
20 fresh asparagus tips	noodles
1/4 cup freshly grated	3/4 cup heavy cream
parmesan cheese	1/2 pound smoked salmon,
1 teaspoon capers	cubed
additional parmesan cheese	

1. In a 2 quart skillet over medium heat, place wine, noodles, asparagus, cheese and cream. Bring to a boil, then reduce heat to simmer. Add salmon and capers just long enough for salmon to be slightly broken. Portion onto four dinner plates and sprinkle with parmesan cheese.

J's Fresh Seafood Restaurant

Dinner for Six

Shrimp and Pasta

Pasta Salad

Salmon En Croute with Pink Cream Sauce

Amaretto Mousse

Wine:

With the Salmon - Far Niente,
Nappa Valley Chardonnay, 1985
With the Mousse - Chandon Brut Reserve Champagne

J's Fresh Seafood Restaurant

J's Fresh Seafood Restaurant is conveniently located in the center of Cincinnati, in Hyde Park, an upscale residential area located just minutes from downtown Cincinnati. J's occupies the bottom floor of the Regency, a condominium highrise, impeccably maintained inside and out.

J's Seafood Restaurant has been in the Cincinnati area for just 7 short years, but in those years has earned the reputation of one of the finest dining spots in this city of great restaurants. In fact a recent poll in Cincinnati Magazine voted J's one of the top three restaurants in the city... and gave J's the very select honor of being rated a "Hall of Fame" restaurant.

J's name gives you some insight to their specialties, but does not really tell the whole story. Only fresh seafood is a must at J's... swordfish, sole, shrimp, lobster, crab, mussels, scallops. But J's doesn't stop there, you can also enjoy prime beef from Chicago, lamb, chicken and some of the most creative pasta dishes you'll ever see.

About two years ago J's began featuring an "Italian Night" every Wednesday and Thursday. Along with their regular menu, J's features a number of special Italian entrees... plus, the most fantastic fresh antipasti table. This has earned J's the title of Best Italian Restaurant three years in a row, not bad for a two night a week menu.

The secret to success for this award-winning restaurant... Jimmy Gherardi, a legitimate food genius. Jimmy owns the restaurant, and has kept an eye over it for all 7 years. Jimmy has an uncompromising attitude toward food quality and service. Greater Cincinnati's Restauranteur of the Year in 1987, Jimmy Gherardi spends endless hours making sure that his customers receive the very best in food and service.

The next time you're looking for a classy restaurant, with a cozy little bar... a great wine list... "Award Winning Service"... and an outstanding menu, try J's Seafood Restaurant — then you'll understand what all the awards are about!

2444 Madison Road
Hyde Park
(513) 871-2888

Shrimp and Pasta

12 large shrimp, (peel
  and devein)
2 tablespoons fresh diced
  basil
1 teaspoon salt and pepper

4 oz. olive oil
2 tablespoons fresh diced
  garlic
2 cups chopped tomatoes
2 boxes Buitoni vermicelli

1. Cook the vermicelli and put to the side. Add all ingredients in a saute pan and cook until the shrimp are done. Then add the vermicelli and serve.

Pasta Salad

Salad:
1 cup broccoli
1 cup mushrooms
2 heads lettuce

1 cup cauliflower
1 cup carrots
2 cups pasta shells
1 cup tomatoes

1. Cook pasta shell, and then clean the lettuce. Chop the vegetables and combine in a large bowl. Mix well. Then add the dressing to coat the vegetables, pasta and lettuce.

Dressing:
1 quart salad oil
1 tablespoon granulated
  garlic
1/2 pound granulated sugar
1 cup red wine vinegar

4 egg yolks
1 tablespoon granulated
  onion
1 teaspoon cracked black
  pepper

1. Using a food processor, process egg yolks, onion, garlic, pepper 1/2 cup vinegar. Add half of the salad oil very slowly. Add sugar and rest of red wine vinegar. Add rest of salad oil.

Salmon En Croute with Pink Cream Sauce
1 Fillet of Salmon
Puff Pastry
Mushrooms (chopped)

Sauce:
1 tablespoon tomato paste
1/4 cup white wine

1 quart heavy cream
1/4 cup fish stock

1. Roll out puff pastry. Skin the salmon. Place mushrooms on pastry, then place salmon on mushrooms. Pull the pastry on top and put small holes in pastry. Bake until pastry is brown at 340 degrees for 15-20 minutes.
2. Reduce stock, then reduce wine. Add paste and cream, cook until sauce becomes thick. Serve with salmon en croute.

Serve with seasonal vegetables. Enjoy!

Amaretto Mousse

10 oz. Amaretto Liqueur
8 egg yolks
20 oz. whipped cream (scaled
   out before whipping)

4 oz. confectionar's sugar
2 oz. orange juice concentrate

1. Combine Amaretto, sugar, egg yolks, and orange juice in either a double boiler or heavy guage pot. Heat and stir frequently with a wire whip until mix becomes slightly custard-like and thick. (About 20-30 minutes.) When slightly thickened, remove from heat and strain through a small - medium hole strainer. Allow to cool in refrigerator.
2. Whip cream to a soft peak. Combine Amaretto mix with whipped cream. (Fold in with a spatula! Not a whip!) Puree praline mix in food processor. Portion into glasses or bowls, and sprinkle praline over top as desired. Enjoy!

Praline Topping Mix

1/2 cup toasted almonds
1 cup pecans
1 tablespoon sugar

La Normandie

Dinner for Six

Caesar Salad

Blackened Tenderloin

Billy Xander

Wine:

Zinfandel, Nalle 1986

La Normandie

A downtown Cincinnati tradition for over 50 years. Famous for dry-aged steaks, fresh fish and a selection of other hearty fare that reflects a long-standing dedication to the sheer joy of eating and drinking. Daily specials are prepared with sauces spirited from the Maisonette kitchen. Located downstairs under the brick archway next to The Maisonette and historically popular with the city's business community and local celebrities. Happy Hour occurs daily Monday through Friday in the cozy bar where you throw peanut shells on the floor and the great hors d'oeuvres are on the house. Live piano entertainment nightly, free parking at Walnut Garage for dinner. Lunch Monday through Friday; dinner Monday through Saturday. Major credit cards.

118 East Sixth Street
(513) 721-2761

Caesar Salad
Dressing

1 cup olive oil
1 tablespoon Dijon mustard
1 tablespoon anchovy puree
1-1/2 teaspoons Lea & Perrins

1/4 cup red wine vinegar
1 egg yolk
1 teaspoon chopped garlic
salt and pepper to taste

1. Blend together the egg yolk, mustard, anchovy puree, garlic and Lea & Perrins. Add slowly the red wine vinegar. Add slowly the olive oil.

Salad

2 heads Romaine lettuce, cut in long slices (cut off ends and all brown leaves)

4 tablespoons seasoned croutons (diced size)
2 tablespoons grated Romano cheese

Cajun Magic Spice Mix

10 tablespoons salt
2 tablespoons black pepper
4-1/2 teaspoons white pepper
1 tablespoon Gumbo File
3 tablespoons paprika
4-1/2 teaspoons chili powder

3 tablespoons garlic powder
2 tablespoons cayenne pepper
1 tablespoon ground oregano
4 tablespoons onion powder

Note: This recipe makes a large quantity of Spice Mix, La Normandie suggests storing it in an airtight container for future use.

Blackened Tenderloin
6 Fillets

1. Dip top and bottom of fillet in Spice Mix.
   If you use a cast-iron skillet:
     - Heat skillet on high for at least 40 minutes.
     - After spice, dip each side of fillet in peanut oil.
     - Place fillet in pan for 1 - 2 minutes on each side or until blackened.
   If you use a flat top:
     - Heat flat top on high for 40 minutes
     - After spice, place fillet directly on flat top for 1 - 2 minutes each side.
2. Finish cooking under broiler, on a flat pan. Top with pepper butter star.

Jalepeno Butter

1 fresh jalepeno (medium)   *1/4 pound butter*

1. Roast or saute jalepeno - peel and seed. Mix into butter in a buffalo chopper or cuisinart. Pipe into stars and refrigerate.

Billy Xander
(Dessert Drink for One)

1/2 oz. rum   *3/4 oz. dark cream de cacao*
1 scoop ice cream   *1/2 oz. half and half*
1/2 scoop of crushed ice   *1 oz. bittersweet sauce*

Lenhardt's

Dinner for Four

Goulash Soup

Hungarian Paprika Schnitzel

Creamed Broccoli

Linzer Torte

Lenhardt's

Lenhardt's restaurant started in 1955 at 201 W. McMillan Street, by Anton and Emmi Lenhardt, and Kristoff and Anni Lenhardt. The capacity was about 26 seats. In 1958 the Restaurant grew into the Dry Cleaning store next door and 60 seats with an expanded menu of Austro-Hungarian, German and American Cookery.

In 1964 Anton Lenhardt purchased the Moerlein Estate at 151 W. McMillan and converted it into the present Restaurant with a larger menu consisting of 11 different Veal Schnitzels, Sauerbraten and Potato Pancake, Kassier Rippchen and Sauerkraut, Hungarian Goulash, Chicken Paprikasch and also American Foods.

The Austro-Hungarian Desserts, baked by Erika, include the famous Dobosch Torte (9 layers), Mocha Almond, Strudels, Chocolate Hazel Nut, Almond Torte filled with Fresh Strawberries and Fresh Whipped Cream, Cheese Cake and many other Tortes.

In 1977 Anton and Emmi Lenhardt retired. Their daughter Erika and (Joe) W.H. Windholtz became the owners of Lenhardt's. Parking at the corner of Clifton and McMillan was added in 1978. Mobil rating of Three Stars 1983, 1984, 1985. Two Stars 1986. Lenhardt's remains in the Tradition and Quality of the Original.

151 West McMillan Street
(513) 281-3600

Goulash Soup

3-4 pounds meaty veal bones
1/2 medium onion, chopped
2 teaspoons fresh parsley,
  chopped
1-2 tablespoons butter
1 tablespoon flour
1 tablespoon good paprika
1/2 cup flour
1 large potato, peeled and cut
  in 1/2 inch dice

2 ribs celery, diced
1/2 cup carrot, chopped
1/2 pound boneless veal,
  cut in 1/2" cubes
1/2 medium onion, grated
salt and pepper to taste
1 egg
1 teaspoon water

1. In a large heavy kettle, place the veal bones and cover with water. Bring to a boil, then add the celery, chopped onion, carrot and parsley. Bring back to boiling, then reduce heat and simmer about two hours. Skim surface foam frequently.

2. In another kettle, brown the veal cubes in the butter. Stir in the grated onion. Then stir in 1 tablespoon flour, stirring constantly until smooth. Salt and pepper to taste. Remove kettle from heat and stir in paprika. Pour the broth through a strainer and stir strained broth into meat kettle. Slowly bring to a boil.

3. Meanwhile, in a small bowl, stir together the egg, 1/2 cup flour and water until smooth. Using the spoon edge to cut pieces of this dumpling dough into rectangles about one-fourth by three-fourths inch, drop into the boiling soup. Add the cubed potato. Reduce heat and simmer about 5-10 minutes until potato is tender.

Hungarian Paprika Schnitzel

(This recipe serves one, however, it may be increased to serve more - but do not crowd skillet or even browning will not occur.)

1/4 cup all purpose flour	*1 teaspoon salt*
1 tablespoon vegetable	*4 veal scallops (2 oz. each)*
shortening	*3 tablespoons water*
1 teaspoon paprika	*1 small onion, sliced*
1/3 cup heavy cream	

1. On a small shallow plate, mix flour and salt. Melt shortening and heat. Dust scallops lightly with flour mixture and brown in skillet over medium heat. When one side is drowned, add sliced onion, brown other side, add the water. Stir lightly to dissolve the drippings and form natural sauce, add cream and cook until thick.

2. Serve on a warmed plate, top with a dill pickle, and garnish with a dollop of sour cream and fresh parsley. *This arrangement displays the colors of the Hungarian Flag.

Creamed Broccoli

1 bunch broccoli	*1/2 cup unsalted butter*
1/2 cup flour	*1/2 cup milk*
1/2 cup heavy cream	*1/2 cup fine dry bread crumbs*

1. Steam broccoli until tender-crisp and place in a baking or gratin dish.

Rue:

Melt butter, sift in flour, cook until set. Stir in warm milk until blended, add cream, pour over steamed broccoli and sprinkle bread crumbs over top. Place in a preheated 400 degree oven for 5-8 minutes - until cream is bubbly.

Linzer Torte

1 cup unsalted butter,
  softened
1-1/2 cups sugar
grated peel of one lemon

2 cups sifted cake flour
3 cups ground almonds
2 eggs
1 tablespoon cinnamon

1 cup red current jelly, excellent quality, at room temperature

1. This dough must be made by hand. The quality will be affected if a mixer or food processor is used. In a large mixing bowl combine the butter and flour until well mixed. Using a wooden spoon, stir in the almonds, sugar, eggs, lemon peel and cinnamon. Mix well until a dough forms.

2. Butter well and then dust with flour a nine inch round cake or loose bottomed deep tart pan. Using 3/4 of the dough, pat evenly on bottom of pan building up sides slightly. Chill remaining dough. Spread the jelly atop dough.

3. Roll out remaining dough between sheets of waxed paper for easier handling. Then make lattice strips decoratively across top of torte. Place in a preheated 350 degree oven and bake 1 hour and 15 minutes. Cool completely on a rack. Remove sides if using loose bottomed pan.

Maisonette

Poached Shrimp & Scallops on Leaf Spinach
Sauce of Setchuan Pepper, Mustard and Cream

Salade de Fromage de Chevre

Veal with Tomato & Basil

White Chocolate Mousse

Wine:

With the Seafood: Muscat, Klack 1985
With the Salade: Simi Rosé of Cabernet 1986
With the Veal: Gamble Chardonnay 1983
With the Mousse: Möet & Chandon N.V.
(non Vintage) Brut

Maisonette

Truly world class. One of only ten restaurants in America, and the only one in Cincinnati, currently meriting Mobil's prized Five-Star Award: "One of the best restaurants in the country," (so acclaimed for 24 consecutive years). Accolades include the Travel/ Holiday Magazine award (33 consecutive years) and recognition in Tradition & Qualite's worldwide guide to French dining (one of just seven American restaurants). An international staff creates and presents classic French cuisine in an elegant, tranquil setting. The proprietors personally select the extensive wine list to reflect changing tastes and values from around the world. A treasure of fine paintings graces the walls and adds to the lovely ambience. The reputation for flawless, sophisticated service is a Maisonette trademark. Close to all downtown hotels. Call for reservations. Jackets and ties for gentlemen. Lunch served Monday through Friday; dinner, Monday through Saturday. Closed Sunday and holidays. Valet parking during dinner hours. Major credit cards.

114 East Sixth Street
(513) 721-2260

Poached Shrimp & Scallops on Leaf Spinach —
Sauce of Setchuan Pepper, Mustard and Cream

2 large raw shrimp, peeled and
   deveined (2 oz. total)
3 oz. fresh leaf spinach,
   parboiled
1 teaspoon French mustard
1/2 fresh tomato, seeded,
   peeled and finely diced

3 medium fresh scallops
   (3 oz. total)
1/2 teaspoon crushed
   Setchuan pepper
2 oz. heavy cream
3 oz. fish stock

1. Cook shrimp and scallops in fish stock - remove and keep warm. Bring cooking liquid to boil - reduce to half its volume. Add tomato, mustard, pepper and cream. Reduce until the sauce thickens slightly. Strain through a fine strainer.
2. Arrange the warm leaf spinach in the center of the plate. Place the scallops and the shrimp on top of the spinach. Pour the sauce on top of the seafood.

Salade de Fromage de Chevre

2 small goat cheese diced
2 Belgian endives
1 large sweet red pepper,
  broiled, peeled and sliced
  in thin strips

2 heads Bibb lettuce
1 small head Romaine
  (heart only)
mustard vinaigrette with fine
  herbs

Vinaigrette

3 soup spoons olive oil
1 teaspoon Dijon mustard
1 soup spoon finely chopped
  herbs (tarragon, parsley and
  chives in equal portions)

2 soup spoons red wine
  vinegar
salt and pepper to taste

1. In a large bowl arrange the mixed Bibb and Romaine leaves in center, the Belgian endive all around. Place the diced cheese and strips of red pepper in center. Season with salt and pepper. Just before serving, add the vinaigrette. Mix well.

Veal with Tomato and Basil
(Serves Four)

4 6 oz. veal steaks
4 ripe tomatoes, peeled, seeded
  and diced
1 soup spoon fresh chopped
  parsley
2 soup spoons olive oil
juice of 1 lime

4 oz. sweet butter
1 oz. chopped fresh shallots
8 fresh basil leaves, thinly
  sliced
4 slices of eggplant, (1 inch
  thick, 2 inches in diameter)
salt and pepper

1. Heat the olive oil in a heavy skillet. Add the tomato, shallots, parsley and basil. Season with salt and pepper. Cook slowly until almost dry - keep warm. Cook veal steaks in 2 oz. butter until golden brown - remove. In the same skillet add the rest of the butter - let foam. Cook briefly the eggplant slices which have been lightly dipped in flour. Season with salt and pepper.

2. Arrange the tomato preparation in small mounds on each plate. Top it with the slice of eggplant. Arrange the veal steak along the side of the tomato. Pour the lime juice on the veal. Serve hot.

White Chocolate Mousse

12 oz. white chocolate
4 egg whites
4 oz. powdered sugar
few drops vanilla

8 oz. light karo syrup
4 oz. granulated sugar
1 quart whipping cream

1. Melt chocolate slowly and completely. Stir in syrup. Whip egg whites to stiff peak. Halfway through, add granulated sugar. Beat until all granules disappear.
2. Fold into chocolate - syrup mixture until completely mixed. Whip cream, vanilla and sugar very stiff. Fold into above.

Bittersweet Sauce

Melt 1 pound bittersweet chocolate.
Add 1 cup 40% cream or half and half.

National Exemplar

Dinner for Five

Crabcakes

Caesar Salad

Italian Stuffed Chicken

Pineapple Sorbet

National Exemplar

The National Exemplar Restaurant is located in the historic village of Mariemont. Set in the tudor style Mariemont Inn, the Exemplar has the unique ambiance of a Country Inn. Enjoy the pub with its hardwood floors and cushioned booths or the dining room with a cozy fireplace.

Breakfast promises fluffy omelettes, oversized pancakes, and many creative egg dishes. Homemade pastas, dry aged steaks, the freshest seafood, and daily blackboard specials are featured nightly.

6880 Wooster Pike
Mariemont Inn
(513) 271-2103

Crabcakes

1/2 pound crab
1/4 cup bread crumbs
1 egg
1 tablespoon minced onion
1 tablespoon mayonaise
1 teaspoon Dijon mustard

1 teaspoon Worcestershire
  sauce
1/2 teaspoon tabasco sauce
1/2 teaspoon salt
1/4 teaspoon pepper

1. Mix in 3 ounce patties. Coat each patty in crumbs before cooking. Saute until brown, turning frequently, approximately 5-10 minutes.

Caesar Salad

1 tin of anchovies
1/4 jar Grey Poupon mustard
1 tablespoon black pepper

4 cloves garlic, finely minced
1-1/4 cups white vinegar
4 cups salad oil

1. In mixer, blend cloves, anchovies, mustard, pepper, salad oil, and lastly white vinegar for approximately 5 minutes. Toss with romaine lettuce, fresh parmesan cheese, and croutons.

Italian Stuffed Chicken

5 boneless breasts of
  chicken
Mozzerella cheese

2 tablespoons fresh pesto
1 piece prosciuto ham, thinly
  sliced

1. Stuff chicken with pesto, ham and cheese. Close with toothpick and cook at 350 degrees for 25 minutes.

Pineapple Sorbet

1/2 can unsweetened
  pineapple juice
1/8 cup Gran Marnier

simple syrup
juice of 2 lemons

1. Cuisinart 1/2 can pineapple juice, lemon juice, simple syrup, Grand Marnier. Pour into shallow pan and freeze. When frozen, recuisinart and freeze again.

Newport Beach

Dinner for Two

Tequila Burre Blanc

Veal Medallions

Raspberry Crepe

Newport Beach

The owners of the five-star Maisonette have created the new rave on the river - a spectacular entertainment and dining complex. The Newport Beach dining room offers the romance of river dining with breathtaking views from every seat. Graceful, flawless service compliments the extraordinary menu, featuring such regional American specialties as Kentucky Chicken Breast grilled over a wood fire with apples, bacon and cider butter, Rack of Lamb with fresh herbs and Grilled Norwegian Salmon with kiwi barbecue sauce. The raw bar is outstanding. The extensive wine list reflects the proprietors' personal selections from around the world. Inside at the Bar or outside at SPLASH enjoy the area's most diverse collection of musical talent from rock to blues to jazz. The Bar's sliding ceiling lets you dance beneath the stars. The atmosphere is casual and fun; the food is light and fresh.

301 Riverboat Row
Newport
(606) 581-9000

Tequila Burre Blanc
Marinate

6 large shrimp peeled and
  deveined
1 tablespoon lime juice
2 tablespoons tequila

1 teaspoon garlic, minced
sprig of cilantro
1 tablespoon olive oil

Burre Blanc

1 shallot
sprig cilantro
1/2 oz. lime juice
pinch of pepper
2 oz. whole butter sweet
5 pieces diced red pepper
garnish

1 clove garlic
1 oz. tequila
pinch of salt
4 oz. reduced cream
2 oz. honeydew and cantalope,
  julienned

1. Marinate shrimp, herbs and liquid. Prepare Burre Blanc sauce - reduce cream with shallots, garlic, cilantro, lime, salt and pepper. Whip in reduced tequila. Whip in butter.
2. Saute shrimp in butter. Arrange on plate - top with sauce. Garnish in center of plate, with cantalope, honeydew and diced red apple, cilantro leaf on final circle.

Veal Medallions

*4 - 2-1/2 oz. portion to be seasoned with salt, pepper,
fresh herb mix of rosemary, thyme, basil and flour.
Saute in 1 oz. of clarified butter*

Basil Pinot Noir Sauce

1. Saute shallots, bay leaf, fresh thyme and cracked black pepper.
2. Add 2 cups wine to deglaze the pan and reduce by 2/3. Strain through a cheese cloth and add chopped fresh basil.
3. Add 1 quart of veal stock and continue to reduce. To finish sauce, whip in 2 tablespoons of butter.

   Place veal on hot plate and top with sauce. Garnish with carmelized shallots and 1 fresh basil leaf.

Carmelized Shallots

1. Saute shallots in butter. Salt and pepper to taste. Keep shallots moving in pan, approximately 8 minutes. Add 1 fresh basil leaf.

Raspberry Crepe
(for one)

1 crepe
2 oz. pastry creme
1/2 oz. Grand Marnier
whipped cream
1-1/2 oz. creme aungalse

3 oz. raspberries
1 tablespoon powdered sugar
cinnamon
1-1/2 oz. raspberry sauce

1. Place 1-1/2 oz. of creme aungalse sauce on one side, 1-1/2 oz. of the rasberry sauce on the opposite side of a chilled white plate with crepe. Put in pastry creme, raspberries and fold. Spray crepe with grand Marnier. Powder one side of crepe with sugar; powder one side of crepe with cinnamon. Pipe whipped cream onto the top and serve.

Orchids
At The Palm Court

Dinner for Six

Grilled Salmon Fillet
Served on Tomato Mint Vinaigrette

Salad of Bibb, Endive, and Raddichio
Champagne Vinaigrette and Fresh Nasturtiums

Intermezzo of Fresh Papaya Sorbet

Sauteed Medallions of Beef, Lamb and Veal
Served on Cassis Butter Sauce and Topped with Forest Mushrooms

Poached Floating Island
Chilled and Served on Raspberry Coulis

Freshly Brewed Coffee

Chocolate Truffles

Wine:

*With the Salmon - Mayacamus Chardonnay,
Napa, 1985*

With the Salad - Saratoga Sparkling Water

*With the Medallions - Beaulieu Private Reserve,
Georges de Latour, Napa, 1981*

*Menu Prepared by: Joseph Emanuelli -
Executive Sous Chef*

Orchids

O rchids, located in the restored French art deco Omni Netherland Plaza Hotel, represents the finest in American dining. The
restaurant opened five years ago in 1983, and has positioned
itself as one of Cincinnati's most reputable dining rooms.

Chef Damian Reolon, Executive Chef, creates the seasonal menu of beef,
lamb, seafood and game, and presents them in spectacular fashion. The
Swiss born chef has traveled extensively and has pleased the palates
of thousands across the world. The chef's talented staff is completely
guest oriented and continually strives to achieve 100% guest satisfaction.
Orchids prides itself on delivering gracious and impeccable service in
elegant and stunning surroundings. The dining rooms boast Brazilian
rosewood walls, 14 karat gold and silver sconces and a 75 foot mural
ceiling which takes you back in time.

35 West Fifth Street, (513) 421-1772
Chef Damian Reolon, Executive Chef Omni Netherland Plaza Hotel
Craig Pishotti, Orchids Manager
Gene McMenamin, Director of Food and Beverage
Omni Netherland Plaza Hotel

Grilled Salmon Fillet
Served on Tomato Mint Vinaigrette

6 3 oz. Alaskan King or
Norwegian salmon fillets
6 large beef steak tomatoes,
peeled, seeded and diced
salt and pepper to taste

5 oz. salad oil
1 bunch fresh mint
2 limes
5 shallots, finely chopped

1. Marinate salmon in 4 oz. of salad oil with half a bunch of the mint (finely chopped). Peel and seed the tomatoes. Dice into 1/2 inch pieces and place in a stainless steel bowl. Grate the rind of the two limes into the tomatoes until the entire rind is removed and then cut the lime in half and add the juice of the limes to the tomatoes. Remove 6 sprigs of the remaining mint for garnish and set aside. Finely chop the remaining mint and add to the bowl. Peel and finely chop the shallots and add to the bowl. Season with salt and pepper.
2. Prepare a very hot and clean grill. Remove salmon from marinade and allow for the excess oil to drain off. Place salmon on grill and cook two to three minutes per side. Salmon should be slightly under-done in center in order to maintain moisture. While salmon is cooking, place an even amount of the tomato mint vinaigrette in the center of each plate. Place watercress around the tomato mixture. Remove salmon from grill and place on center of plate atop the tomatoes. Place sprig of mint atop each salmon fillet for garnish.

Salad of Bibb, Endive and Raddichio
Champagne Vinaigrette and Fresh Nasturtiums

2 heads hydroponic bibb or
Boston lettuce
3 shallots
1 bunch fresh chives
2 egg yolks

2 heads Belgian endive
1 head red Raddichio
5 oz. champagne
salt and pepper
6-12 orange or red edible
Nasturtiums

1. Clean all lettuce with cold water and let dry. Lay the bibb on the plates first at the top of the plate (about 3 to 4 leaves). Place two Raddichio leaves so that they are halfway covering the bibb. Place 4-5 endive leaves pointing out from the Raddichio so to cover the ends of the endive. This can be done up to three hours in advance if they are covered.

2. In a stainless steel bowl whip the 2 egg yolks until airy. Add the shallots (finely chopped) and then proceed to add the oil slowly. Briskly whisk the eggs in order to incorporate the oil thoroughly. After half of the oil has been added add all the champagne. The dressing will look slightly watery at this point, but that's O.K. Next, continue to add the rest of the oil in the same manner as before and the dressing begins to thicken. Season with salt and pepper and add the chopped chives. Add dressing to salad, about 2-3 oz. per serving. Serve immediately.

Papaya Sorbet

5 ripe papaya
20 oz. water
1 pint strawberries

14 oz. sugar (granulated)
3 egg whites

1. Obtain a home ice cream maker (I recommend the Donvier - 1/2 gallon machine). Freeze the ice cream canister for one whole day. Peel and de-seed papaya. Reserve 3 halves for garnish. After papaya has been cleaned, puree in food processor and set aside. Combine 14 oz. sugar and 20 oz. of water together in a sauce pan and bring to a boil. This will totally dissolve the sugar. Remove from heat and let cool. Add the three egg whites to the sugar mixture and combine well. Add the pureed papaya and mix well. Place entire mixture into the ice cream canister and mix according to your machine's directions. Once sorbet is made, store in freezer until ready to use.

2. Take remaining three halves of papaya and cut in half again thus giving you six wedges. Place each wedge on a small plate and surround with sliced strawberries. Scoop sorbet and place in papaya wedge. Serve immediately.

Sauteed Medallions of Beef, Lamb and Veal
Served on Cassis Butter Sauce and Topped with Forest Mushrooms

*6 2 oz. beef medallions (from
the tenderloin)*
*6 2 oz. lamb medallions (from
the lamb loin)*
1 bottle Creme de Cassis
6 oz. fresh currants (optional)

*6 2 oz. veal medallions (from
the tenderloin of ribeye)*
*1 pound sweet butter,
softened*
*1-1/2 pounds sliced shitake
mushrooms*

Sauce:
Peel and finely chop shallots. Saute over medium heat in 1/2 oz. of butter until soft. Add entire bottle of Creme de Cassis and cook over high heat until reduced to about 5 oz. Remove from heat and briskly whip in all the remaining butter (ounce by ounce) until thoroughly incorporated. Season with salt and pepper and place sauce in a double boiler and cook over low heat.

Meat:
Season meats with salt and pepper. Saute meats in a large skillet over high heat for two minutes each side (for medium rare). While the meat is cooking saute the sliced shitake mushrooms and shallots in butter over high heat for three minutes or until soft. Season with salt and pepper. Once mushrooms are cooked, place 4 oz. of cassis butter sauce on a plate. Lay the medallions of meat on the sauce and top with shitake mushrooms. Sprinkle with currants. Garnish plate with steamed baby vegetables and serve.

Poached Floating Island

5 egg whites
2 tablespoons cream of tartar
6 sprigs of mint
3 oz. Grand Marnier

5 oz. sugar (granulated)
1 pint fresh raspberries
4 oz. butter

1. Mix egg white, sugar and cream of tartar together in an electric mixing bowl and whip until stiff peaks.
2. Completely butter six coffee cups. Add whipped egg whites to each cup (3/4 full). Place cup in a water bath and poach in oven at 350 degrees for 18 minutes. To check to see if they are done, stick toothpick in and pull out - if the toothpick comes out clean they are ready. Let stand and cool. DO NOT REFRIGERATE.
3. While cooling, take one pint of raspberries and puree in a blender or food processor until smooth, then add Grand Marnier. Place 2 oz. of raspberry coulis on plate. Place poached egg white on top of coulis and garnish with a sprig of mint. The coulis can be made up to two days in advance. The floating island can be made up to four hours in advance.

Pigall's
French Restaurant

Dinner for Four

Coquilles Saint-Jacques `a la Provencale

Cream d'Asperges

Red Leaf and Watercress Salad

Loin de Veau à L'Épinard et au Fromage de Chevre

Sauce de Madere

Tart au Citron

Wine:

With the Coquilles: Chardonnay or Sauvignon Blanc
With the Loin de Veau: Cabernet Sauvignon
or Pinot Noir
With the Dessert: "Late Harvest" - Johannisberg
Riesling or Champagne

Pigall's

Fonde 1956
Eight Mobil Five-Star Awards
Fourteen Mobil Four-Star Awards
Thirty-Two Travel / Holiday Awards

A Cincinnati landmark of tradition, style and good taste. The diner is surrounded by elegant intimacy. A stained glass window depicting the seal of Paris establishes its national origin. The main dining area has exquisite chandeliers that cast reflections in the smoky mirrors on the sidewalls, and a mural of a Paris street scene provides a "window" for the rear. As the guests enter through the wrought iron and glass door, you can hear "Oh How Lovely", they do appreciate the Parisian feeling. Owner Donald G. Whittle is ever ready to recommend an appropriate wine or to invite guests to visit The Cave, one of the country's prized wine cellars.

127 West 4th Street, (513) 721-1345

Coquilles Saint-Jacques à la Provencale

15 to 18 large sea scallops
2 oz. flour
3 tablespoons butter
2 garlic cloves, peeled and
  minced
1/2 cup dry white wine
1 large tomato, peeled,
  seeded and diced

salt and pepper to taste
3 tablespoons oil
1/3 pound white mushrooms,
  sliced
1 lemon
2 shallots, minced
1 tablespoon chopped parsley

1. Wash scallops well in salted water, pat dry on paper towel. Season the scallops and dust with flour.
2. In a large skillet, heat the oil and butter. Saute the scallops on high heat until they are lightly golden on both sides. Remove from skillet, keep warm.
3. Add mushrooms to skillet, saute for 2 minutes, add garlic, shallots, tomatoes, juice from 1 lemon, white wine, simmer for 2 minutes, pour over scallops, sprinkle parsley over top.

Crème d'Asperges

1/2 pound fresh asparagus
1-1/2 oz. diced onions
1 quart chicken stock
salt and pepper to taste
dash of nutmeg

3 oz. unsalted butter
1-1/2 oz. flour
8 oz. heavy cream
1/2 cup dry white wine

1. Wash asparagus, cut into one inch pieces, keep the tips separated from the other pieces.
2. Melt the butter in a soup pot, add the onions and cook until transparent. Add the asparagus pieces (not the tips), dash with flour, stir thoroughly, pour in the chicken stock, stir and bring to a boil. Simmer for about 30 minutes over low heat.
3. Place in a blender and puree until smooth, then strain through a wire strainer back into the soup pot, bring to a boil. Add the asparagus tips, simmer for 2 minutes, add cream, wine, nutmeg.

Red Leaf and Watercress Salad

2 tablespoons white wine
    vinegar
6 tablespoons olive oil
1 small head of red leaf
    lettuce, separated into leaves,
    rinsed and dried
2 hard boiled eggs - large

1 teaspoon Dijon mustard
1 teaspoon fresh or dried
    tarragon, chopped
2 bunches of watercress,
    stems discarded, leaves
    rinsed and dried

1. In a small bowl, whisk together the vinegar, mustard, tarragon, and salt and pepper to taste. Add the oil in a stream, whisking, and whisk the dressing until it is emulsified.
2. Line the salad plates with red leaf lettuce, place watercress in a salad bowl and toss with the dressing, place on top of leaf lettuce. Separate egg yolks from white, and sieve them on top of salad.

Loin de Veau à L'Épinard et au Fromage de Chevre
Sauce de Madere

1/2 veal loin (4 pounds)
1 oz. butter
1 oz. shallot, chopped
salt and pepper
2 oz. Maderia

1/2 pound fresh spinach
1/2 pound goat cheese, mild,
  such as Montrachet
16 oz. brown veal stock

1. Trim the loin, save the bones and trimming for the veal stock. Split the loin lengthwise, butterfly style, season inside of the loin with salt and pepper.
2. Saute spinach in butter with shallots for two minutes, let cool. Spread spinach over loin, crumble cheese, and sprinkle along center of loin. Roll the loin and tie firmly with string. Season the outside of the loin with salt and pepper.
3. Roast for one hour at 350 degrees until meat is still pink inside. (Do Not Over Cook) Remove veal from the oven, place on platter. Deglaze pan with Maderia and veal stock. Simmer for 15 minutes, skim the fat. Strain and pour around veal after slicing. Garnish with glazed carrots.

Brown Veal Stock

4 oz. vegetable oil
2 carrots, chopped
2 stalks celery, chopped
1 clove garlic, chopped
3 oz. tomato paste
4 oz. dry white wine
1 teaspoon dry thyme

veal bones and skins,
  chopped and cut in
  small pieces
1 large onion, chopped
2 fresh tomatoes, chopped
2 quarts water
3 bay leaves

1. Heat roasting pan, add bones and trimmings, place in a pre-heated oven and roast at 350 degrees for about 1 hour or until brown. Add carrots, onion, celery. Continue roasting for 15 minutes, add tomatoes, tomato paste, garlic, mix. Add water, wine, spices, stir and mix well.
2. Bring to a boil, lower heat and simmer for about 2 hours, skimming off the fat occasionally. Strain through a cheese cloth.

Tart Au Citron

Pastry

1-1/4 cup flour
7 tablespoons sweet butter
2-3 tablespoons water

1/4 cup granulated sugar
pinch of salt

1. Cream together the butter and sugar. Add the flour, salt and mix until dough forms a ball. Prepare tart shell and refrigerate.

Lemon Filling

1 cup granulated sugar
7 tablespoons butter, melted
   and luke warm

5 egg yolks
1 orange
3 lemons

1. Beat the sugar and egg yolks until the mixture whitens, add the butter, the zest of one lemon, whisking well, pour in the juice of the three lemons and one orange and continue to beat until thoroughly combined.
2. Pour in the prepared tart shell, and set in a preheated 350 degree oven to bake about 30 minutes. Serve luke warm or cool. Just before serving dust with confectionery sugar.

Rusconi's Galeria

Dinner for Six

French Onion Soup

Spinach Salad with Hot Bacon Dressing

The Michael Angelo

Strawberry Gateau

Rusconi's Galeria

The interior is bright and open, the managers are award-winning industry veterans and the menu features some of the most popular items found on the American scene. This is Rusconi's Galeria.

We are known in Cincinnati as an "anytime" restaurant. A point has been made of making Rusconi's the place where diners can sit quietly and conduct business in our oversized booths, or rush in for a quick late-night drink or meal.

We pride ourselves on our friendly service, large portions of fine food and creative home-made desserts.

126 West Sixth Street
(513) 621-7550
(One block from the Cincinnati Convention Center)

French Onion Soup

3 Bermuda onions
1 cup beef stock
2 tablespoons garlic powder
2 slices provolone cheese
 (each bowl)

1-1/2 cups sherry wine
1 cup butter
1 cup parmesan cheese
 (each bowl)
4 oz. croutons (each bowl)

1. Julienne Bermuda onions and saute in butter until golden brown. Combine with four quarts water. To this mixture add beef stock, sherry wine and garlic powder. Simmer for 30 minutes.

2. Laddle into bowl, add croutons, place provolone cheese on top, sprinkle with parmesan cheese and place under broiler. Heat until cheese becomes golden. Garnish with parsley and serve immediately.

Spinach Salad with Hot Bacon Dressing

Salad

2 pounds spinach leaves
2 medium Bermuda onions,
 sliced in thin rings

1-1/2 pounds mushrooms
6 hard boiled eggs

1. Wash spinach leaves. Arrange on plate topped with sliced mushrooms, onion and hard boiled egg. Pour the hot bacon dressing over top of spinach and serve.

Dressing

18 strips of bacon
1 cup red wine

1 cup white vinegar
1 cup sugar

1. Pan fry bacon, take bacon drippings, add vinegar, red wine, sugar and boil until mixture becomes syrupy. Chop the bacon and add to mixture.

The Michael Angelo

6 oz. fettuccine noodles
4 oz. garlic butter
3 bay scallops
4 oz. baby shrimp
4 oz. garlic butter
1 piece parsley

4 oz. white wine
4 pieces jumbo shrimp
2-2 oz. pieces of cod
4 oz. white wine
1 slice jack cheese
1 lemon wedge

Note: Ingredients are broken down to one serving in order to ensure ease of cooking.

1. In skillet heat 4 oz. white wine, 4 oz. garlic butter (per serving). Saute jumbo shrimp, scallops, cod and baby shrimp. Next add more white wine (4 oz.) and garlic butter (4 oz.). Put in casserole dish on 6 oz. of cooked noodles. Put jack cheese on top and melt in broiler. Place lemon wedge and parsley on a plate under casserole dish.

Strawberry Gateau

Pastry Dough

8 cups flour
4 cups water
1/2 cup baking powder

6 eggs
2 cups sugar

1. Mix 8 cups flour, 6 eggs, 4 cups of water, 2 cups sugar and 1/2 cup baking powder in large bowl at one time. Fill pastry bag and squeeze out onto cookie sheet into the form of a donut. Bake at 350 degrees for 15 minutes or until golden brown. Let cool for 5 minutes. Slice lengthwise to form two halves. Clean and cut strawberries, place half of them on one half of pastry dough.

Filling

1 pint strawberries
4 tablespoons vanilla
1 cup sugar

1 quart heavy whipping
cream

1. In bowl mix 1 quart whipping cream with gradual amounts of the one cup of sugar and four tablespoons of vanilla extract. Whip until thick. Place half of this mixture into pastry bag and add a layer of this over the strawberries. Add another layer of strawberries on top of filling and take remaining filling and dispense over second layer of strawberries.
2. Place other half of pastry shell on top, sprinkle the whole donut ring with powdered sugar, pour chocolate syrup gingerly over powdered sugar. Cut into separate servings and serve.

Shield's Crossing

Dinner for Four

Mussels Farcie Bretonne

Italian Endive Soup

Tomato and Avocado Vinaigrette

Paupiettes of Chicken Breasts Calvados

Buttery Lemon Mousse

Shield's Crossing

S hield's Crossing offers the perfect setting for your dining pleasure and your holiday party. The nostalgic history dates back to Edward Shield himself - a personality well known in the Cincinnati area as a leader and member of many active groups.

Mr. Shield's home was a gathering place for his family and many friends where good food and drink were greatly enjoyed. Today the tradition is carried on in a manner befitting his original style of hospitality.

Join those who come from miles around who have discovered the uniqueness of Shield's Crossing - circa 1868 - spacious lawns, towering ancient trees, period gazebo and fountain. But the food is the thing! Unique and marvelous! Fresh seafood, salads, soups and desserts. Created for your pleasure - served in spacious rooms or on the veranda overlooking the garden. Fine wines and cocktails. Listed on the National Historic Register.

220 Riverside Drive
Loveland
(513) 683-8220

Mussels Farcie Bretonne

*4 dozen small Blue Mussels,
scrubbed well and debearded
1/2 cup dry white wine
2 tablespoons onion, chopped
1 tablespoon garlic, chopped
salt and pepper to taste*

*2 tablespoons butter
1/4 cup bread crumbs
2 tablespoons parsley,
chopped
2 tablespoons parmesan
cheese*

1. Saute onion and garlic in butter until golden. Add mussels and wine and cover to steam for about 5 minutes or until all are opened. (Discard any unopened shells). Remove mussels to a serving platter and keep warm.
2. To wine and juices in pan, add bread crumbs, parmesan cheese and chopped parsley, (sauce should be slightly thickened). Season with salt and pepper to taste and pour or spoon over mussels. Serve with plenty of French bread.

Italian Endive Soup

2 quarts chicken stock
1 slice salt pork
1 rib celery with leaves
1/2 carrot
1/2 onion
2 cloves garlic
salt and pepper

4 sprigs parsley
1 tablespoon olive oil
1 small can Italian plum
  tomatoes
1 large bunch curly endive
2 eggs, beaten
grated parmesan cheese

1. Make "battuto" by chopping salt pork, celery, carrot, onion, garlic and parsley to a paste (or a processor may be used). Saute battuto in olive oil in soup pot over medium heat until fat is rendered and vegetables are limp.
2. Add stock and chopped plum tomatoes with their juices. Bring to a simmer and cook for 10 minutes. Add chopped endive and cook for 5 minutes. Stir in beaten eggs. Salt and pepper to taste and serve with grated parmesan cheese.

Tomato and Avocado Vinaigrette

3 Avocados
red leaf lettuce or ornamental
   Kale

2 large tomatoes
black olives

1. Half avocados and slice each half lengthwise into six sections. Slice tomatoes and cut slices into halves. Arrange avocados and tomatoes in pinwheel arrangement on lettuce. Garnish with olives and serve with Vinaigrette dressing.

Vinaigrette

2 cloves garlic
1/2 cup oil
3 tablespoons wine vinegar

1 teaspoon Dijon mustard
1 spring parsley
salt and pepper

1. Put garlic, mustard, parsley and salt and pepper (to taste) in blender. With machine running, slowly add oil until well blended.

Paupiettes of Chicken Breasts Calvados

4 boneless chicken breasts
   pounded 1/4" thick and cut
   in half
1/4 cup thyme
5 tablespoons butter
1/2 cup onion
1 cup tart apples, peeled and
   diced

1/2 cup bread crumbs
1/4 teaspoon poultry
   seasoning
1/2 teaspoon salt
1/8 teaspoon pepper
vegetable oil to fry
1 large clove garlic

1. Saute onions, garlic and apples in butter and add bread crumbs and seasonings. Stuff chicken breasts, roll up (tucking in ends) and secure with toothpicks.
2. Saute until lightly browned and bake in 325 degree oven for 20 minutes. Serve with Calvados Sauce and wild rice.

Calvados Sauce

1 cup heavy cream
1/3 cup apple cider

1/3 cup calvados
salt and white pepper to taste

1. Bring all ingredients to a simmer and cook for approximately 5 minutes, or reduce to about 1 cup.

Buttery Lemon Mousse

3/4 cup sugar
juice of 2 lemons
rind of 1 lemon, grated

1/4 cup butter
3 eggs, beaten
1 cup whipped cream

1. Mix together sugar, juice and rind. Melt butter in double boiler over simmering water. Add sugar mixture and beaten eggs and cook until thickened - about 5 minutes. Refrigerate until cool and fold in whipped cream. Garnish with lemon curl and fresh mint.

Top of the Crown

Barbecued Shrimp

Golden Onion Soup

Grilled Vegetable Salad with Salad Burnet Vinaigrette

Alaskan King Salmon with Yogurt & Cucumber Sauce

Baby Vegetable Saute

Herb Roasted New Potatoes

Dill Soda Bread with Parmesan Butter

Raspberry Brie

Wine:

with the appetizer - Fume Blanc, Robert Mondavi
(also great with Brucks Beer)
with the entree - Chardonnay, Cakebread
with dessert - Chenin Blanc, Dry, Calaway

Debbie G. Goulding - Chef

J. David Gulley - Matre D'

The Top of the Crown is a combination of fresh, innovative American cuisine, 3-star dining elegance and a comfortable decor that helps every guest feel at home. Add to this one of the best views of the Cincinnati skyline and you have the ingredients for an exceptional dining experience.

"There are three requirements for every dish that leaves our kitchen - fresh, fresh and fresh." Chef Debbie Goulding insists on nothing less. "I love fresh herbs - and we use many different kinds in combinations which, I think, enhances the flavor of the best American dishes."

Goulding makes a point to introduce innovative entrees and appetizers on a regular basis, to make sure there's always a delicious alternative for the returning guest. The chef also has introduced several "light" entrees for the calorie-conscious guest.

Goulding and her staff find that "the Top" is often the setting for special occasions such as birthdays and engagements. "With some advance notice, we've helped arrange for special flowers at the table. We've even helped the groom-to-be by hiding the ring in a flower arrangement to add an additional surprise to the evening."

The atmosphere at the Top is restrained and in keeping with the newly redecorated dining room and lounge areas. Guests will find an abundance of green plants, subdued, tasteful upholstery and carpets, plus service that's attentive yet never overbearing.

Regular patrons of the Top of the Crown often come back for its signature dishes such as it Steak Diane, which is prepared tableside. And the Top's Caesar Salad won the "Award of Excellence" in the 1988 Taste of Cincinnati.

And then there is the view.

Whether you prefer a river view or a city view, every table is afforded both from the Clarion's 31st floor, as the restaurant makes a leisurely turn during your meal. "Every evening begins with a new and beautiful sunset. It's a perfect setting for a relaxing dining experience," says Chef Goulding. Add to this the strains of Shirley Jester at the piano and the experience is complete.

Fresh, innovative, comfortable. The Top of the Crown takes the best of fine American cuisine and adds all the right touches to ensure a relaxed atmosphere that makes dining as their guests a delicious and complete pleasure.

141 West Sixth Street   Robert R. Hoeb, General Manager
(513) 352-2100   David Saxton, Executive Chef

Barbecued Shrimp

24 shrimp (large), peeled and
  deveined
3 limes, juice
2 tablespoons Cajun seasoning

1/2 pound butter (unsalted)
2 tablespoons Worcestershire
1 cup white wine
1/2 cup garlic

1. In skillet melt butter and add Worcestershire, lime juice, white wine and Cajun seasoning. Cook over medium heat for 15 minutes to reduce and then add shrimp.
2. Cook shrimp until pink, approximately 6-8 minutes. Add chives and toss. Remove from heat and serve immediately. Serve with plenty of French bread to dip in sauce.

Cajun Seasoning

1/2 cup cayenne pepper
2 tablespoons garlic powder
2 tablespoons oregano, ground
2 tablespoons basil, ground

2 tablespoons black pepper,
  ground
2 tablespoons thyme, ground

1. Combine thoroughly and store in tightly covered can or jar. *This mixture can also be used for blackening food.

Golden Onion Soup

5 medium onions, 4 sliced thin
  and 1 pureed
4 cups chicken stock
1/2 cup sherry

8 pearl onions
4 tablespoons unsalted butter
  (melted)
4 green onion tops, chopped

1. In saucepan, melt butter and add onions. Cook slowly for 20-30 minutes, stirring occasionally until carmelized (deep golden brown).
2. Add chicken stock and cook for 1 hour on medium heat. Stir in sherry and add pearl onions. Cook for 15 minutes. Sprinkle with green onions.

Grilled Vegetable Salad with Salad Burnet Vinaigrette

1 pound spinach leaves
1 green bell pepper
1 medium zucchini, cut
  quarters (lengthwise)
1 small eggplant, cut in 1/2
  inch slices
8 medium mushrooms
1-1/2 cups olive oil

1 red bell pepper
1 yellow bell pepper
2 red pear tomatoes, cut
  in half
4 large green onions
4 small red onions (Maui or
  Vidalia if available)

1. In broiler pan, roast peppers until skins are black on all sides. Imediately seal in a plastic bag and put in freezer until cool. When peppers are cool, remove from freezer and peel away skin. Pull out stems to remove seeds, careful to save juices for vinaigrette.
2. Blanch zucchini and eggplant for 5 minutes in hot water and cool with ice water. Cut peppers in four pieces each.
3. Cut red onion 1 inch down from top several times in crisscross manner, so to form mum. Arrange vegetables in single layer on lightly oiled grill rack. Brush with olive oil. Making sure charcoal is very hot, position rack 3 inches from coals and brush vegetables with olive oil.
4. Cook vegetables for 5-7 minutes turning occasionally until lightly browned. Remove vegetables from grill and arrange on spinach. Serve with Salad Burnet Vinaigrette.

Salad Burnet Vinaigrette

1 cup olive oil
1 tablespoon garlic, finely
  chopped
1 tablespoon green onions,
  finely chopped
1 tablespoon black pepper,
  freshly ground

1/4 cup red vine vinegar
1 tablespoon shallots, finely
  chopped
*1/3 cup *Salad Burnet,*
  chopped
2 tablespoons bell pepper
  juice (optional)

1. Combine all except oil in processor and process for 2 minutes. Add oil and blend 2 minutes more. Let stand at least 1 hour to blend flavors. *Salad Burnet is an herb that has the taste of cucumber.

Alaskan King Salmon with Yogurt and Cucumber Sauce

*4-8 oz. Alaskan King Salmon
  fillets, skinned
2 tablespoons lemon juice,
  freshly squeezed*

*1/2 cup butter (unsalted)
  melted
2 tablespoons white wine*

1. Arrange fish (skin side down) on baking sheet and add butter, lemon juice and wine. Bake at 400 degrees for 10-12 minutes until firm to touch. Serve topped with yogurt and cucumber sauce. Garnish with sprig of fresh spearmint.

Yogurt and Cucumber Sauce

*8 oz. yogurt, plain
8 seedless cucumber, peeled
  and cut in 1 inch pieces*

*1 tablespoon garlic, chopped
  fine
2 tablespoons spearmint,
  chopped fine*

1. In processor, chop cucumber until fine (but not pureed). In bowl, combine yogurt, garlic, cucumber and mint. Refrigerate for at least 2 hours before serving.

Baby Vegetable Saute

8 baby yellow pear tomatoes
4 red pearl onions, peeled
4 baby leeks, stem trimmed
12 Enoki mushrooms
3/4 cup butter (unsalted),
  melted
2 tablespoons lemon juice,
  freshly squeezed
1 tablespoon opal basil,
  chopped fine

4 white pearl onions, peeled
4 baby white eggplant
4 sunburst squash, cut in half
4 large flowering savoy
  leaves
2 tablespoons white wine
1 tablespoon lemon zest
1 tablespoon lemon thyme,
  chopped fine
1 tablespoon garlic, chopped
  fine

1. Blanch pearl onions and leeks in hot water for 5 minutes and rinse with ice water. In saute pan, combine butter, white wine, lemon juice and zest, lemon thyme, opal basil and garlic.
2. Add tomatoes, pearl onions, leeks, eggplant and squash. Saute 6 minutes and remove from heat. Arrange vegetables on savoy leaves and top with Enoki mushrooms.

Herb Roasted New Potatoes

12 new potatoes (approx. 2-3")
2 tablespoons rosemary, leaves
  stripped from stems
2 cups olive oil

2 tablespoons sage, chopped
  fine
2 tablespoons garlic, chopped
  fine

1. Peel strip around center of potato. Cook potatoes in boiling water for 15 minutes and pour off water. Arrange in baking dish and add oil and herbs, stirring to coat. Bake at 400 degrees for 30 minutes or until golden brown.

Dill Soda Bread

2 cups bread flour*
1/2 teaspoon baking soda
1/2 teaspoon salt
2-1/2 tablespoons vegetable oil
3/4 cup buttermilk, at room
 temperature

1/2 teaspoon double acting
 baking powder
2 tablespoons dill, freshly
 chopped

1. Position a rack in the top third of oven and preheat at 350 degrees. In a large bowl, combine flour, baking powder, baking soda, salt and dill. Combine oil and buttermilk in separate bowl. While stirring with wooden spoon, slowly pour buttermilk mixture into flour mixture. Mix well until dough forms a ball.

2. Place dough on lightly floured work surface. Knead dough for about 5 minutes, adding additional flour, if necessary to form a moist, smooth dough. Place on ungreased baking sheet. Bake for about 45 minutes, or until loaf sounds hollow when tapped on the bottom with your fingers. Cool loaf on wire rack. Serve warm, but not hot, or at room temperature with parmesan butter.
   *Bread flour is a high-gluten flour available in most stores.

Parmesan Butter

1/2 pound butter (unsalted),
 soft

1/4 cup parmesan cheese,
 grated fine

1. Combine thoroughly. Make rosettes or put in small dishes to mold. Refrigerate until serving time.

Raspberry Brie

4 rounds Brie cheese
   (4-1/2 oz. rounds)
1/2 box Filo dough
1 cup butter (unsalted),
   melted

1/2 cup raspberry preserves
2 tablespoons Chambord
   liqueur

1. Trim rinds completely from Brie rounds and set aside. In small bowl, combine Chambord and preserves, set aside. Cut roll of filo in half (cover remaining half and return to refrigerator or freezer for future use).
2. Carefully separate sheet of filo and lay out flat on work area. Brush filo lightly with butter, making sure all corners are covered. (Keep roll completely covered, as to make sure it does not dry out, while you're working on each sheet.) Repeat with three more sheets, layering one on top of each other.
3. Turn stack of four sheets over and brush again with butter. Place Brie in bottom half of sheets, top with two tablespoons of raspberry mixture. Fold filo over Brie from bottom half first, tucking in the sides and continue folding until closed like an envelope.
4. Put on buttered baking sheet and bake in oven at 350 degrees for 15-20 minutes until lightly browned. Serve with Lavosh crackers or fruit.